D1541681

Getting
Into
COMPUTERS

Getting
Into
COMPUTERS

By Kurt Hanks

WARNING Once in, you may
never get out!

 **DATAMOST**

20660 Nordhoff Street, Chatsworth, CA 91311-6152
(818) 709-1202

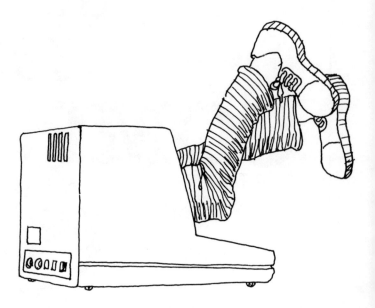

⊕ DATAMOST™

ISBN 0-88190-395-7

Printed in U.S.A.

WARNING:
The Sturgeon* General Has Determined That Computers Are Dangerous to the Status Quo.

* Sounds fishy to me, too.

A GREAT BIG THANKS!

As in the creation of any scholarly publication, a writer learns that it would have been impossible to have written it alone. It is a lot of work from the faltering beginnings until you read this sentence. And many people shared in that work. Here they are and a great big thanks to them:

TABLE OF CONTENTS

Absolutely, positively, everything you would ever want to know about personal computers is in this book. If you can't find it in here, you don't want to know about it. And here is where it all is:

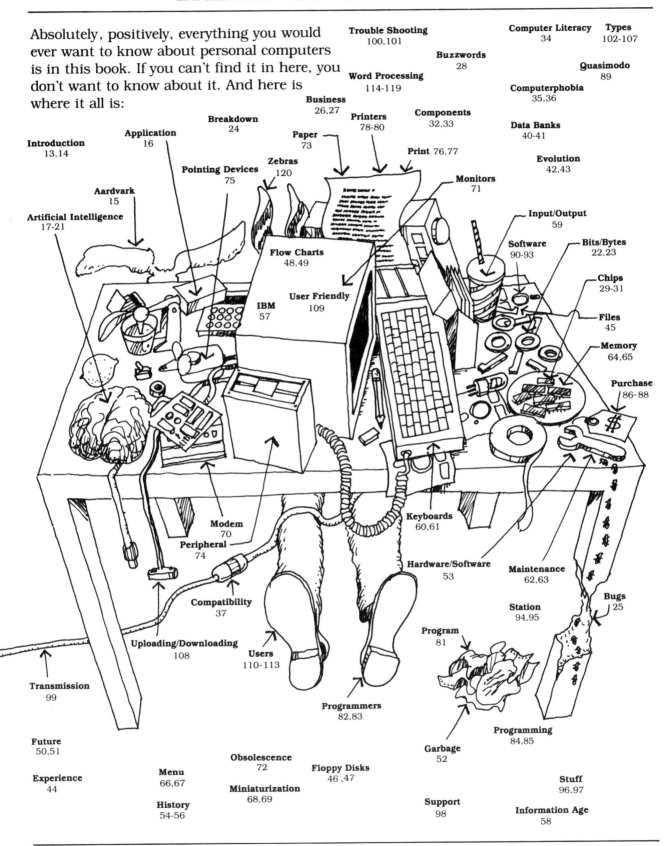

Trouble Shooting
100,101

Buzzwords
28

Word Processing
114-119

Business
26,27

Computer Literacy
34

Types
102-107

Quasimodo
89

Computerphobia
35,36

Breakdown
24

Printers
78-80

Components
32,33

Data Banks
40-41

Introduction
13,14

Application
16

Paper
73

Print 76,77

Evolution
42,43

Pointing Devices
75

Zebras
120

Monitors
71

Aardvark
15

Input/Output
59

Artificial Intelligence
17-21

Software
90-93

Bits/Bytes
22,23

Flow Charts
48,49

Chips
29-31

User Friendly
109

IBM
57

Files
45

Memory
64,65

Purchase
86-88

Modem
70

Keyboards
60,61

Peripheral
74

Hardware/Software
53

Maintenance
62,63

Compatibility
37

Station
94,95

Bugs
25

Uploading/Downloading
108

Program
81

Users
110-113

Transmission
99

Programmers
82,83

Programming
84,85

Future
50,51

Garbage
52

Experience
44

Menu
66,67

Obsolescence
72

Floppy Disks
46,47

Stuff
96,97

Miniaturization
68,69

History
54-56

Support
98

Information Age
58

If you can't find it here, try the index on page **123**.

BEGINNING A JOURNEY

 Some people fear computers as a technological plague that will eventually consume the economy, their job, and finally even themselves. They see the future as a flip-flop on today, where people are the slaves and computers are the masters.

Many more people fear the computer as a nameless threat they can't put their finger on. They feel the computer, by some mysterious process, knows more than they do. It even knows their weaknesses and, if it so pleases, the machine can use that knowledge against them.

Still more people fear that merely touching a computer will break the machine. It can never be fixed after this murderous act with a finger, but in its last spasm will flash the culprit's name endlessly across the screen.

Then there is the growing number of people who have lost the fear of computers. To them the computer is just another tool. It is like a hammer or a typewriter. It is smart and very quick, but still only a tool to be used by them and for them. Their life has been greatly improved by having a computer and knowing how to use it.

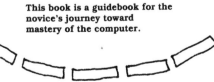

This book is a guidebook for the novice's journey toward mastery of the computer.

A wimp of a person, cowering to a mechanism they should control.

See note: 2

The gap between these two extremes, one of fear and the other of competence, involves a journey. This is a guidebook for that journey.

The proud master of a tool he uses for a better life.

See note: 1

Note 1: For some strange reason this group is made up of a large number of runny-nosed kids.

Note 2: This group is largely made up of otherwise competent adults.

HOW TO USE THIS BOOK

To help you in getting the most out of this book, I've included this page as a guide. Following these helpful hints can greatly improve your enjoyment and learning levels. Please read this page carefully.

Defend Yourself by using this book in arguments over various computer systems.

Shed Some Light with this book on the different possibilities opening up through computers.

Alphabetical Order for your quick and selective access. Key points on software and hardware are featured throughout. Here is an alphabet. Sing it with that little song we all learned in elementary school and you can easily find your way.

A B C D E F G H I J K L M N O P Q R S T U V W X Y Z

Fill Up Your Open Mind with this book on new computer technology and what it will mean to you.

Stand Out in any crowd by using copies of this book.

Give this book to the novice.

Multiple Copies are available from the same place you got this one.

3 SECRETS EVERY AARDVARK MUST KNOW WHEN HE REACHES PUBERTY

Learning these three secrets is a major milestone in every little aardvark's life and will be in yours if you want to suck-up ants. So, read carefully the following material:

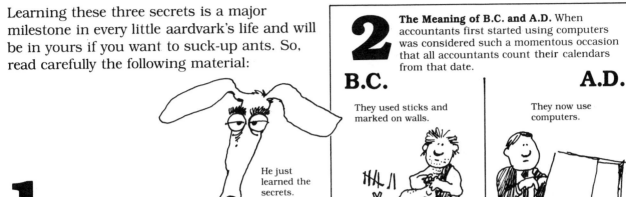

He just learned the secrets.

1

The Definition for Computer Failure to learn this means you will be ostracized from the group. You will be considered out-of-it and a definite nerd.

2

The Meaning of B.C. and A.D. When accountants first started using computers was considered such a momentous occasion that all accountants count their calendars from that date.

B.C.

They used sticks and marked on walls.

B.C. means **B**efore **C**omputers.

A.D.

They now use computers.

A.D. means **A**fter **D**ata processing.

3

The First Personal Computer Steven Jobs, the founder of Apple Computers, called his machines *Personal Computers* and started the whole mad rush.*

Have a byte.

Eve had the first computer. She had an Apple. Adam had the second computer. He had an Apple II.

---

* They weren't the first microcomputers, but Jobs capitalized on the term *Personal Computer*.

A COMPUTER'S MARRIAGE WITH OTHER TECHNOLOGY

Computers are beginning to run things. What used to take our control or the control of some technical professional is now being done by a computer. This trend is expected not only to continue, but to drastically speed up.

Computers are appearing in things: like toys, carburetors, motors, and wallets. We are allowing the installation of silicon brain power in places that took people brain power before.

With this insertion of computer intelligence in controlling our existing technology, there will be a corresponding increase in efficiency.

Existing Technology   The Computer   Newer, Better Technology

Computers give us a cheap way to intelligently control things, for example:

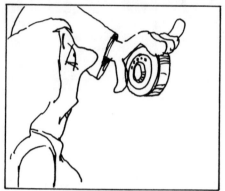

You could stand by a thermostat, adjusting the temperature as needed, even turning things off at night, and your gas bill would go down. But you wouldn't get any sleep and would end up with an unbelievable back pain.

Now you can get a computerized thermostat and it will regulate the temperature.

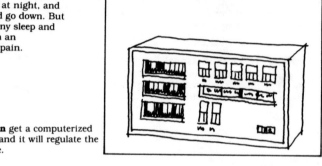

You could hire an automobile mechanic to hold on to the front of your car as you drive and adjust the carburetor (if you can find one dumb enough) to save gas. But if he bills you, you won't be able to afford shoes, let alone a car.

Now you can buy a car with a computer that constantly adjusts the carburetor for the greatest fuel efficiency at any one time.

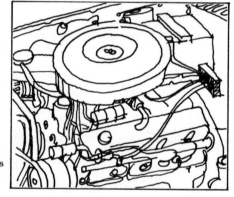

You could have a secretary stay around all the time to remember and call numbers for you and to take messages, which is OK if you enjoy paying for a living shadow.

Now you can get a phone to call numbers for you, record messages, and more.

Computers will fuse so much with other technology, they will disappear. You won't know they are there.

DOC-IN-A-BOX

Walter has got to wearing suits nowadays.

No human contact is ever made.

Anything his little heart desires is available for only a few dollars.

To call Walter, no-Einstein, is one gross understatement. It was an extreme act of mercy when they gave him his high school diploma. I think all he ever really wanted to do was return to the womb, but not being able to do that he chose second best. He stays around home living the life of mama's-little-baby-boy.

But then things began to happen. First he gave stock market advice to his Uncle Howard, advice that proved absolutely correct. Then he told his cousin, Nelda, what had been causing her discomfort weeks before she visited the clinic in Chicago. And still another thing he did was give his neighbor a receipe for crepes suzette that she can't stop raving about. The list of Walter's expert advice which keeps proving itself correct is growing larger each day.

You may now be asking yourself, "why the change?", "why sudden insight from such a lug head?" Well, we finally found out and it was in the basement back in the corner behind the fruit shelves.

There on a barrel was the computer he won in a cereal boxtop contest. (It was fourth place prize, the only thing he had ever won.) He was buying some special new programs for that super computer with a little of his mom's social security check.

Those new programs were the key. Each contained the knowledge of a leading expert in a particular area such as law, medicine, or chemistry. It was all on those little disks which Walter had fed into his computer.

It seems he just asked the computer questions and it gave Walter the correct answer. He then proceeded to tell someone what he knew. (You, at least, have to give old Walter the credit for being able to ask the questions.)

Even now, when everything has been found out, it doesn't seem to matter much. His cousin has given up doctors and now sees only Walter. (He bought a new car with the money she had paid him.) His uncle uses Walter to manage his stock portfolio. And Walter's neighbor has him teaching gourmet cooking down at the civic center. There is even talk of a Walter-for-mayor campaign around town. And I've heard of a proposal for a new public office created especially for Walter as town guru or city sage.

Of course this is fiction, but it is rapidly being consumed by fact. The knowledge of some of our leading experts is **now** being transported into the brains of computers.

It is done when a PhD, who is the top in his field, talks with an interviewer called a knowledge engineer. This engineer organizes the doctor's knowledge into a knowledge base and into rules and methodology. The engineer then has that information translated into a computer program which can then be easily accessed by a variety of people.

There are relatively few systems now, but more are being created all the time. Their impact on our culture, economy, and personal lives hasn't yet been estimated. And besides, it's getting much easier to talk to these machines. Even a Walter will soon be able to have a bunch of experts always on hand to answer his questions.

For a quick summary of these new computer systems (called expert systems) turn the page.

EXPERT SYSTEMS AND ARTIFICIAL INTELLIGENCE

Expert systems and computer programs contain the knowledge of human experts written in a codified form. This programming is modeled after the human experts the knowledge is taken from.

Expert systems are involved in the area of artificial intelligence that concerns itself with structuring human knowledge into computer systems to solve problems.

They have been able to equal or better humans even within the same discipline. These systems are being used in finance, medicine, government, and science, to name only a few areas.

The following is a simplified explanation of expert systems:

Symbolic Representation Incorporates the learning of an expert into a computer program. This program is made to process knowlege in symbols, unlike conventional programming. These symbols may represent any kind of object, person, concept, process, or idea.

Instead of the usual conventional procedure of programming in a step-by-step approach, these systems follow a fact, principle, and rule approach.

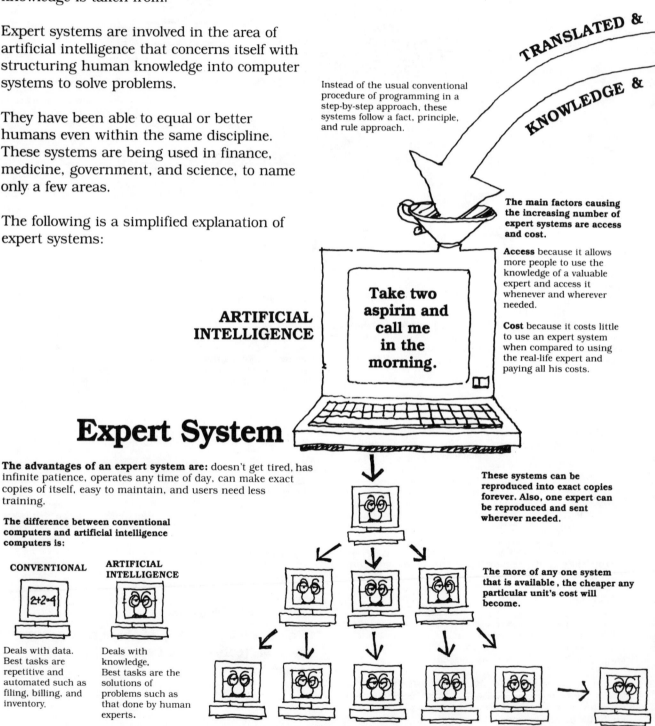

TRANSLATED &

KNOWLEDGE &

The main factors causing the increasing number of expert systems are access and cost.

Access because it allows more people to use the knowledge of a valuable expert and access it whenever and wherever needed.

Cost because it costs little to use an expert system when compared to using the real-life expert and paying all his costs.

ARTIFICIAL INTELLIGENCE

Take two aspirin and call me in the morning.

Expert System

The advantages of an expert system are: doesn't get tired, has infinite patience, operates any time of day, can make exact copies of itself, easy to maintain, and users need less training.

The difference between conventional computers and artificial intelligence computers is:

CONVENTIONAL

2+2=4

Deals with data. Best tasks are repetitive and automated such as filing, billing, and inventory.

ARTIFICIAL INTELLIGENCE

Deals with knowledge. Best tasks are the solutions of problems such as that done by human experts.

These systems can be reproduced into exact copies forever. Also, one expert can be reproduced and sent wherever needed.

The more of any one system that is available, the cheaper any particular unit's cost will become.

Knowledge Engineer - Knowledge Engineering The person who interviews the expert and organizes the knowledge into rules, principles, and data which is then put into computer language is called a Knowledge Engineer. (Honest) The process of converting this knowledge into computer programs is called Knowledge Engineering.

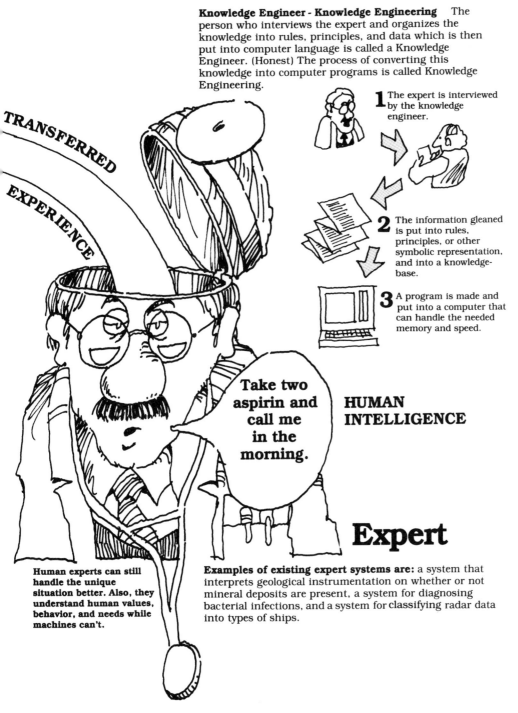

1 The expert is interviewed by the knowledge engineer.

2 The information gleaned is put into rules, principles, or other symbolic representation, and into a knowledge-base.

3 A program is made and put into a computer that can handle the needed memory and speed.

Take two aspirin and call me in the morning.

HUMAN INTELLIGENCE

Expert

Human experts can still handle the unique situation better. Also, they understand human values, behavior, and needs while machines can't.

Examples of existing expert systems are: a system that interprets geological instrumentation on whether or not mineral deposits are present, a system for diagnosing bacterial infections, and a system for classifying radar data into types of ships.

Some organizations involved in creating expert systems are: IBM, Xerox, Texas Instruments, Huges Aircraft, a consortium of Japanese companies involved in the 5th generation computer development, DEC, General Electric, Stanford University, MIT, Defense Department, National Institute of Health, Intelligentics, and Teknowledge.

KEY POINTS ON EXPERT SYSTEMS

◆ There is a shortage of knowledge engineers (only 200 nationwide).

◆ New computers with greater speed and larger memories are encouraging the development of expert systems.

◆ Future systems will learn for themselves.

◆ The goal of interfacing with these systems is to converse with them just like a friend.

◆ Future electronic equipment will have the expertise to repair itself built right in.

◆ Payback time for developing these systems is getting shorter and shorter. Some are paid for in weeks.

◆ They took 20 years to develop at the beginning. Now they take an average of five years, but some are taking only months.

◆ Increasingly, computers are taking over the stages of developing these systems. Fewer and fewer people may be needed to create expert systems in the future.

◆ The first systems cost millions to make. They now are in the hundreds of thousands and the price is still dropping.

◆ One day you will be able to walk into a computer store and buy a DOC-IN-A-BOX.

◆ The expert systems languages first developed were hard to use; easier ones are now in operation and development.

◆ Future professionals may face a shortage of work because of the next stage of automation. The first stage automated work, the next stage will automate knowledge and expertise.

These systems are being put into application at an increasing rate.

The two critical breakthroughs that have caused the creation of artificial intelligence are: the ability to represent human knowledge symbolically and the increasing capabilities of computers.

HOW EXPERT SYSTEMS WORK

The objective of these systems is to allow access to the best minds available for people who need to have expert advise.

Here is the basic structure of expert systems:

An expert system's main parts are the knowledge base and the inference engine.

Knowledge Base is a collection of information an expert uses to make a decision. Additional information is usually added to update and enlarge the base.

Workspace is memory set aside to define, describe, and work on the user's problem.

User Now they are a select few, but that is changing. Direct computer linkup with expert systems in on-line data bases is now available. *In other words you can talk over the phone with some limited system now.*

Interfaces translate the system into computer language and into the language of the user.

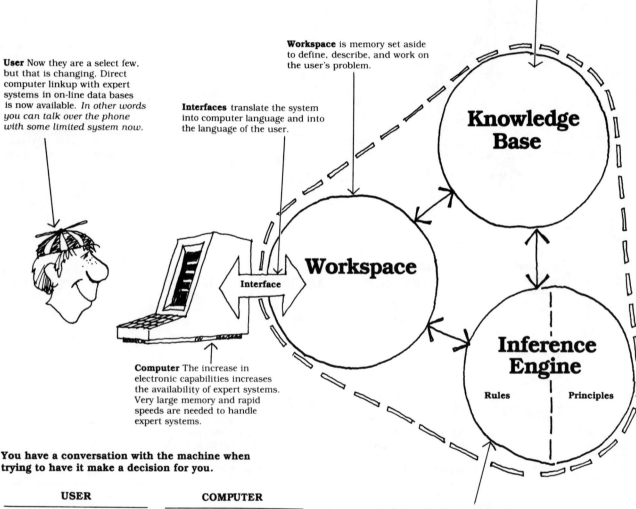

Computer The increase in electronic capabilities increases the availability of expert systems. Very large memory and rapid speeds are needed to handle expert systems.

Inference Engine has two elements: rules and principles. These are used with the knowledge base to solve a particular problem. Some systems may have from 500 to 100,000 rules.

You have a conversation with the machine when trying to have it make a decision for you.

USER	COMPUTER
I'm sick.	What are the symptoms?
I have a high fever, headache, and feel lousy.	How high is your temperature?
101	Does your nose run?
Yes	Swollen glands?
Yes	Anybody else have it?
Yes, little Ralphie had it last week.	You have a cold, take two asprin and interface with me tomorrow.

Principle	Driving an American car is safer.
Rule	**If** you're on a trip **and** are renting a car **then** rent an American car.
Principle	Yellow is the easiest color to see at all times.
Rule	**If** they're painting a fire engine, **then** paint it yellow.

IF COMPUTERS ARE SO SMART, HOW COME THEY ACCEPT MY INPUT?

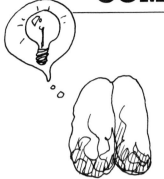

There is a great deal of controversy over whether computers can really think. Do they have intelligence? I think it's just a matter of time before we have one running for political office, at the very least for vice-president. Even if it's not plugged in, the computer couldn't do any worse.

British scientist Alan Turing developed a test to tell if a machine is intelligent. Try it out on your own personal computer. Here is the test:

If you're dealing with a computer and you can't tell whether or not you're talking to a machine or a person, then that is artificial intelligence.

Surprisingly this is starting to happen. For example, read the following true stories:

Cecil Fodwaller as a Dating Game contestant, picked door number 3. He won a date with a Hewlett-Packard HP200.

Mary Jane Kud responded to the computer voice at her local market.

Mickey P. Pulleyfudger is developing a severe dislike for the incompetent people in the billing department at the phone company. He's receiving an automatic computer billing.

Lana Lynn Lowgy thinks she is really talking to Mel Tillis when she receives those telephone solicitations.

Sid Muffin talks to his computer. This is the worst case of all I found.

THE DIFFERENCE BETWEEN A BIT AND A BYTE

According to an *informed source*, "What is the difference "between a bit and a byte?", is the most asked question at White House news conferences. With the administration's permission, here is the answer:

"00000010000101010000110011110011"

Zane Cray
The world's fastest computer

Byte A group of eight bits.

Eight-bit A word size that uses 8 bits.

Sixteen-bit A word size that uses 16 bits.

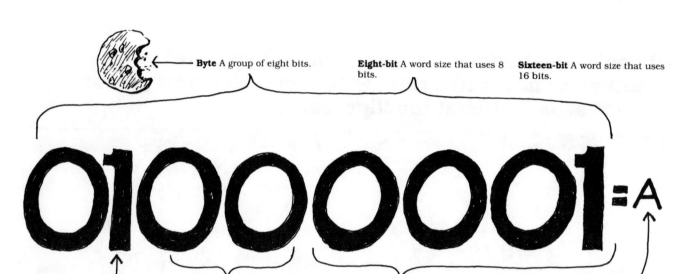

01000001 = A

Bit Binary dig**it** It is the basic unit of computer information consisting of either a 1 (on) or a 0 (off). It takes eight bits to form a character, a punctuation mark, or a symbol.

2 Bits A 0 and a 1 or two 0s or two 1s or a 1 and a 0 or two quarters.

Nibble Four bits or half a byte or something you do to a pretty girl's ear.

Character Symbols, such as letters or numbers, that when arranged into various configurations, like what is on this page, sometimes make sense. Computers can't understand them so they have to translate the characters into sets of binary digits called bits.

Making Sense Bytes are herded together into rows of eight and here, depending on their status (on or off, open or closed, rich or poor) they make a word.

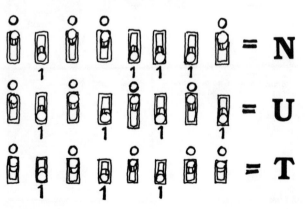

= N

= U

= T

Kilobyte	With computers this doesn't actually represent 1,000, but 1,024. So 1K means 1,024 bytes of data. But THEY round it off to mean an even thousand anyway. 1K
Megabyte	One million bytes of information. 1,000K
Gigabyte	One billion bytes of information. 1,000,000K
Muchobyte	The exact memory of the latest computer on the market that you should have bought.

More And More Memory. These are the common units of memory. We never seem to have enough.

Frankly, Scarlet, I don't give a damn!

9 words, 46 characters, 46 bytes, and 368 bits.

What we have here is a failure to communicate.

7 words, 38 characters, 38 bytes, and 304 bits.

Let me make this perfectly clear.

6 words, 33 characters, 33 bytes, and 264 bits.

For Example: Here are some famous sayings from your favorite characters to illustrate what a bit, byte, or character is.

Bet Your Sweet ASCII Codes American **S**tandard **C**ode for **I**nformation **I**nterchange (Don't you just love all the acronyms in computing?). When you say this acronym, always face East and pronounce it "askee." This is the standard for data transmission that assigns bit codes to a specific set of characters. It is used so that everybody is using the same basic symbols.

Has the typical characters, plus some special ones, too.

The Different Bit Word Sized Machines The higher the bit size, the faster, more capable, and more precise the computer.

8-Bit machine uses an 8-bit word size in its central processing unit.

16-Bit This system uses 16-bit word sizes.

8/16-Bit Their processors work with two eight-bit bytes at a time.

32-Bit This thing is a real hog, it handles two 16-bit word sizes at once.

There are some new and exciting computer products you can buy with bits.

For 4-bits you can buy these distinctive add on ties. Make your computer feel unique.

For 6-bits you can put these little things on your keys to train misdirected pinkies. One box will greatly reduce errors.

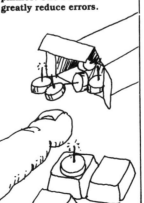

For 8-bits you can buy this. I have no idea what it is, but I'm sure every computer owner should have one for their computer.

THE 3 BIGGEST PROBLEMS CAUSING COMPUTER BREAKDOWN

Even the gem of our technological revolution isn't exempt from the effects of Murphy's Law. I'm sorry to let this out, but computers do break down. They are not the perfect machines we are led to believe.

"The majority of problems we usually have are the obvious things, such as plugging in the computer and loading the software."

Fred Yates
Owner of a computer store

Computer breakdown can be separated into these areas:

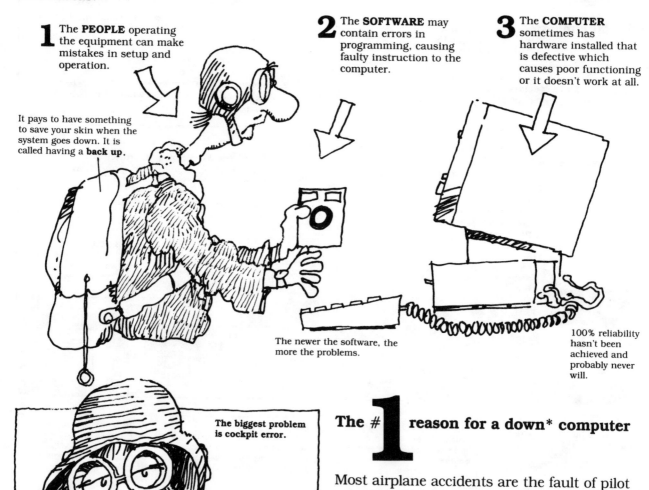

1 The **PEOPLE** operating the equipment can make mistakes in setup and operation.

It pays to have something to save your skin when the system goes down. It is called having a **back up**.

2 The **SOFTWARE** may contain errors in programming, causing faulty instruction to the computer.

The newer the software, the more the problems.

3 The **COMPUTER** sometimes has hardware installed that is defective which causes poor functioning or it doesn't work at all.

100% reliability hasn't been achieved and probably never will.

The biggest problem is cockpit error.

The #**1** reason for a down* computer

Most airplane accidents are the fault of pilot error. The one in the electronic cockpit causes the majority of computer errors also. **Most problems originate in the brain behind the brain.**

The Key Solution

The solution is in knowledge and experience. The more you know, the fewer problems you will have. This applies to flying machines of any kind.

Crash a sudden failure of a computer system.
Down Time The time a computer is down and not working.

* When a computer is down, it is a polite way of saying the blasted machine is busted.

IS YOUR HARDWARE OR SOFTWARE INFESTED?

Being imperfect we always put into what we make a certain degree of that imperfection and computers are no exception. **Computer system mistakes, defects, or malfunctions are called bugs.** The goal is to fumigate and get rid of them. Here are the typical bugs to look out for:

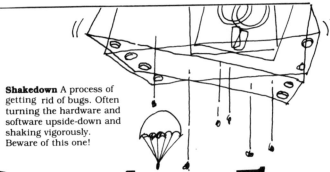

Shakedown A process of getting rid of bugs. Often turning the hardware and software upside-down and shaking vigorously. Beware of this one!

1 **2** **3** **4** **5**

The Logic Bug is when something in the program is out of place. It may be the right instruction, but it's in the wrong place.

The Cosmetic Bugs When the thing works, but it is a messy and over-complicated job.

The Processing Bug When a decimal point is inserted in the wrong place or a hyphen is left out.

The Hardware Bug When the hardware doesn't work. A floppy disk drive is out of alignment or a cable has a short in it.

The First Bug It was a real bug that ate the wiring in the old tube and wire computers.

Here are two common bugs you may want to particularly watch out for:

TICKy-tackey crops up in all sloppy and careless projects.

ArrogANT always appears when you think you have got it licked and every thing is perfect.

Debugging Removing the bugs in the system and restoring it to full operation.

The essential part of the process of removing bugs involves isolating the area where it is located.

If it is not in a definite compartment, a bug is very hard to find even though it often leaves a trail.

But if the system has very separate and distinct parts, you can find the little devil. It's in section M number 3. SQUASH IT!

A	B	C
D	E	F
G	H	I
J	K	L
M	N	O
P	Q	R

Glitch A bug in a business suit.
Debugger System software that searches out and destroys software bugs. It is also a flyswatter.

COMPUTERS FOR BIG BUSINESS

The prime reason to be in business is to make money, whether you're Amalgamated Widgets or Johnny's Lemonade Stand. And one of the biggest problems in either of those businesses is keeping track of that money, where it comes from and where it goes. This is often the difference between success and failure in a business. **Computers excel at keeping track of money.** It does it in the following ways:

Taxes What you owe Uncle Sam can be pulled out automatically in the quarterly reports and at the year end. Johnny owes some sales tax if the city fathers want to be picky about it.

The money goes out here.

Maybe Johnny should use the electronic spreadsheet and see what would happen with costs if he raised prices to a dime a cup.

Loretta hasn't paid anything, but she will cry if Johnny doesn't give her a drink and his stand is on her parent's lawn. A cost of doing business.

Frankie owes 15¢.

Chuck is paid up.

A new customer!

5¢ Johnny's Lemonade

He figured you should buy an Apple if you are running a lemonade stand.

The money comes in here.

The money goes out here.

Accounts Receivable It is the record of the money owed to you. This is where the nourishment comes to keep the business alive. Susan is way past due on that quarter she owes.

The general ledger is now on a disk and it's easy to pull anything off it.

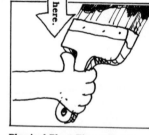

General Ledger It is the basic record keeper for the whole company. It keeps track of how much business you're doing and how you're doing it. Johnny can do spot checks with his computer every once in a while to see how the money and goods are flowing through. He doesn't want things to turn sour on him in the lemonade business.

Physical Plant This software keeps track of the building and equipment. Johnny needs to paint the stand before next month.

Customers This keeps track of your customers, who they are, what they buy and when they buy it. It can also contain their address and phone number. This software can be linked to other related systems, like word processing to send them a card on their birthday. Assisting your customers and cultivating more business from them is critical. Johnny's number one customer is Chuck (chug-a-lug) Jones, and he gets his allowance on Tuesday.

If he stops coming, the business will go downhill.

With a computer you don't need to put in multiple entries. One time, if coded correctly, is all you need to enter it. The computer arranges the entry into the various accounts, doing all the math and filing automatically.

You had better pay up, Johnny. He is threatening to tell Mom.

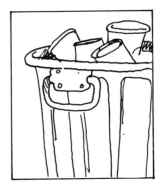

Accounts Payable This keeps track of what you owe others. It is where all the money goes. Johnny has to pay $1.29 to Smith's Market for two cans of frozen lemonade.

Payroll This keeps track of what you pay your employees, their income, deductions, etc. In Johnny's case it is his brother Kevin and he owes him 7¢.

Inventory This keeps tract of what you have back in the warehouse, when to reorder, and how fast things are moving through. Johnny has really been going through the paper cups. He thinks he will just recycle them and use the garbage can as his inventory storage.

Critical information is there at the push of a few buttons. Johnny is the owner and sole proprietor.

The money goes out here.

What If You can project with an electronic spreadsheet and see relationships between various data. As the figures are changed, the program adjusts and recalculates instantly any related data. Johnny is thinking of expanding with other stands, and needs to know what the figures are in each possibility he is considering. A stand down where they are building the new clinic, with all those thirsty construction workers looks the best.

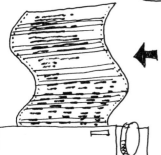

Hardcopy or Printout A printer connected to the computer can give you a paper copy of any data you have, stored away in memory. Johnny has to take a printout of what he needs to invest for future expansion to his dad. If he shows him on Monday, there is no way he can get the money, but Friday is another story.

Business Software The top five business software systems used in computers are: accounts payable, inventory, general ledger, accounts receivable, and payroll. The key points to consider in buying and using these software programs are:

1 Tried and Tested Do they do the job you need and do it the way you want it done. Not what they say they will do, but what they will actually do. The only tried and proven way to find out for sure and not get stuck is to run the software through its paces. Don't do this in the showroom, but in the real world of where you work.

2 Flexibility Most software, I'm sad to say, will never fit your needs exactly. The system must have some flexibility built in. It is going to have to be changed and modified, if not today then for sure tomorrow.

3 Support Services When things go wrong or you've got some unanswered questions, who can you call? That's the big problem with El Cheapo Software; you can't get help when you need it.

4 Cost If it costs you more than you can save in a couple of months then it is probably not worth it. Some of these programs can get quite expensive, but the prices rapidly fall once the newness wears off, demand decreases, and competition appears.

5 Unproven Software Another point to remember is when software first appears it often has errors in it or needs refinements added. If you can wait until all the problems are solved, it would be better to buy a future edition than the new one out now.

USE THE JARGON AND IMPRESS YOUR FRIENDS

Before I learned the secret words, I was a nobody. I had no friends, girls ran away from me, and my dog growled whenever I approached. The day I started using these technical incantations, my world changed. Friends became too numerous to count. Girls threw themselves at my feet. Computer groupies flocked to my every move.

You too can know what fame and success really mean. **Three simple techniques and the world is yours:**

Substitution

Instead of the usual words, insert a computer buzzword or two. You will find your credibility increasing in proportion to the number and length of technical words used and arrogance exhibited.

I've got to go to the bathroom.	I've got to go download.
Going on a date?	Entering the link-up mode?
Read a book.	Scan a data base.
How have you been?	How is the daily operational system?

Initialization

Computer nuts love acronyms. They are sprinkled generously throughout any conversations they have. Season your language with them and bring real power to all you say.

If your memory fails you, just make them up. It will work just as well.

Computer buzzwords can change your life.

You're in an ODE mode, but the ROM will RAS as soon as you begin uploading.

IBM is creating an IC with incredible D/A memory.

When the WAG is operational, the BUS-BUB will glow in the dark.

The latent programmer's eyes brighten whenever his CRT scrolls the FRAN-DAB.

Insertion

This technique is the most powerful one you can use. It is easy to use. All you do is combine the words in one column with any words you choose in the other columns. Any combination of words from the three columns will make miracles.

Word Combination Trick
or
Modulating Syntactic Processor

Interactive	Matix	Architecture
Patterned	Syntactic	System
Symbolic	Integrated	Processor
Inference	Informational	Mode
Diagnostic	Documental	Network
Modulating	Operation	Circuit
Electronic	Binary	Interface
Customized	Synthesizer	Menu
Dedicated	Digital	Simulation
Micro-	Decoder	Debugger
Multi-	Functional	Memory
Quad	Scanning	Language

Before

After

They all laughed when I sat down at the computer—but then I started to input!

...and I thought he couldn't walk and chew gum at the same time.

I wish I were him.

I think I'm in love.

Golly. Neat!

When I grow up I want to be just like him.

Envy & Jealousy

If anyone starts to ask knowing questions concerning what on earth you are talking about, this whole thing is in a **Functionally Inoperable Mode.**

A word of warning is needed. If this is used too often, you will be mobbed and possibly ravaged by adoring fans. Be careful.

MAMA BOLONEY'S FAMOUS CHIP RECIPE

Since all the chip makers have copied her recipe, I can no longer see any reason to keep it a secret. So, here it is:

1 **Cut pure silicon into thinly sliced disks and then cut each disk into 500 little tiny squares.** The silicon crystals must be 99.9999999% pure. It's hard to get, but you can locate it if you shop around. You can also grow your own from raw silicon.

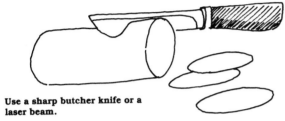

Use a sharp butcher knife or a laser beam.

2 **Draw up a circuit design of your own choosing.** Keep it large so you can get all the circuits you need on it. Have at least 100,000 components drawn on the design.

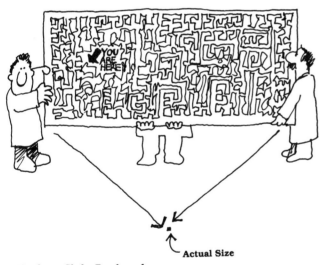

↑ Actual Size

Her boys: Clyde, Frank, and Ezra handle this job.

3 **Reduce the design down to the size of the period at the end of this sentence.** This takes some good camera work and a bucket of patience. Great care should be taken not to sneeze or have the kids open the door.

4 **Lay this period (shrunken circuit design) over a square of silicon and expose to purple light.** A clean kitchen is a must and avoid even a speck of dust. Here is a more detailed set of instructions on what to do:

First heat the silicon in pure oxygen to form a layer of silicon dioxide which conducts electricity.

Second coat the silicon with something (photoresist) that hardens when exposed to light.

Third lay the pattern or mask over it.

Fourth expose it to ultraviolet light.

Fifth wash off all the resist not hardened by the light and throw acid on it to eat away the silicon dioxide that is exposed. Dope, wash, and sprinkle aluminum as need.

Sixth wire and mount into holders. Also test it.

5 **Serve immediately.** Computer companies, electronic game companies, and hardware people gobble these up like chocolate chip cookies. The recipe is always in a state of improvement, you can never get enough circuits onto these things.

TRY ONE!

The people who make the silicon are really called cookers and it's more of an art than a science to grow pure silicon.

A CLOSER LOOK!

If you greatly enlarge a chip, a whole new world is revealed. Shown here, in stages, is an integrated chip magnified many times:

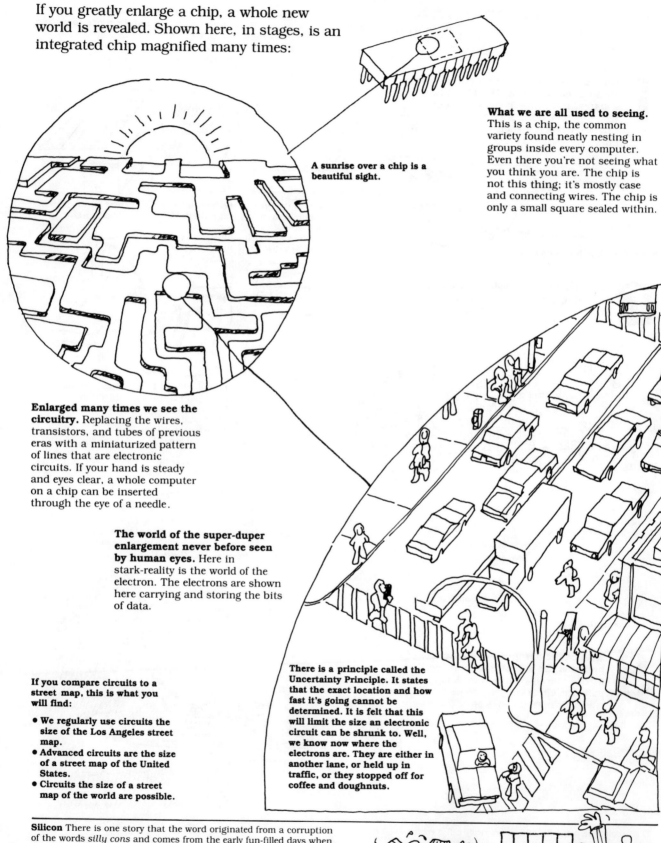

A sunrise over a chip is a beautiful sight.

What we are all used to seeing. This is a chip, the common variety found neatly nesting in groups inside every computer. Even there you're not seeing what you think you are. The chip is not this thing; it's mostly case and connecting wires. The chip is only a small square sealed within.

Enlarged many times we see the circuitry. Replacing the wires, transistors, and tubes of previous eras with a miniaturized pattern of lines that are electronic circuits. If your hand is steady and eyes clear, a whole computer on a chip can be inserted through the eye of a needle.

The world of the super-duper enlargement never before seen by human eyes. Here in stark-reality is the world of the electron. The electrons are shown here carrying and storing the bits of data.

If you compare circuits to a street map, this is what you will find:

- We regularly use circuits the size of the Los Angeles street map.
- Advanced circuits are the size of a street map of the United States.
- Circuits the size of a street map of the world are possible.

There is a principle called the Uncertainty Principle. It states that the exact location and how fast it's going cannot be determined. It is felt that this will limit the size an electronic circuit can be shrunk to. Well, we know now where the electrons are. They are either in another lane, or held up in traffic, or they stopped off for coffee and doughnuts.

Silicon There is one story that the word originated from a corruption of the words *silly cons* and comes from the early fun-filled days when prisoners made the pure stuff.

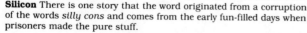

KINDS OF CHIPS

The secret behind computers and why they can do so much are these little things. Whole electronic circuits and even entire computers have been shrunk down to a tiny piece of silicon the size of your fingernail.

Here is a listing of the the main types of computer chips:

ROM CHIP

Can't mess around with what is in it.

ROM **R**ead-**O**nly **M**emory. Can't be altered or written on, only read.

RAM CHIP

When the power is off it forgets everything.

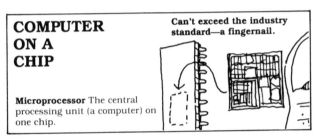

RAM **R**andom-**A**ccess Memory.

Can insert, erase, and read data.

POTATO CHIP

Optional Crinkle Type

Bet you can't use only one.

COMPUTER ON A CHIP

Can't exceed the industry standard—a fingernail.

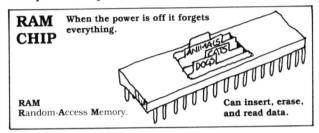

Microprocessor The central processing unit (a computer) on one chip.

CHOCOLATE CHIP

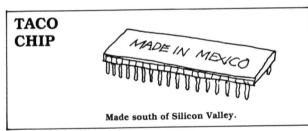

Contains a few delicious bytes.

CUSTOM CHIP

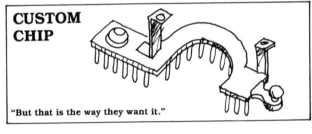

"But that is the way they want it."

TACO CHIP

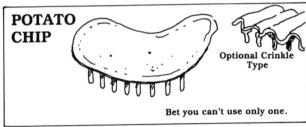

Made south of Silicon Valley.

BUFFALO CHIP

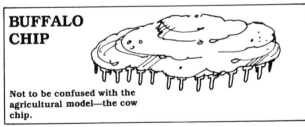

Not to be confused with the agricultural model—the cow chip.

LARGE SCALE CHIP

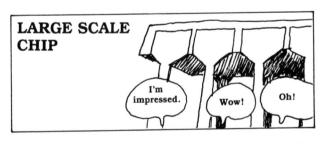

I'm impressed. Wow! Oh!

REJECTED CHIP

SOB! CRY!

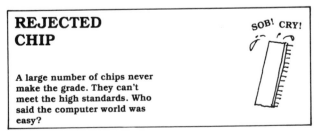

A large number of chips never make the grade. They can't meet the high standards. Who said the computer world was easy?

PROGRAMMABLE CHIP

HEEL!

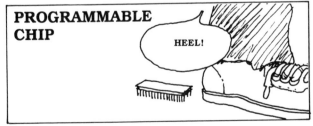

Warning There is a popular misconception that many parts of computers are edible. They are not. But a topical application of any 32K ROM chip to small skin eruptions may prove helpful.

LEAVE IT TO THE BEAVER

And now, ladies and gentlemen, for your reading enjoyment I give you Fred, the trained beaver. Through extensive training, Fred has been certified as a qualified computer disassembler. Here, right before your eyes, **he will take apart an Apple and show you what's inside.**

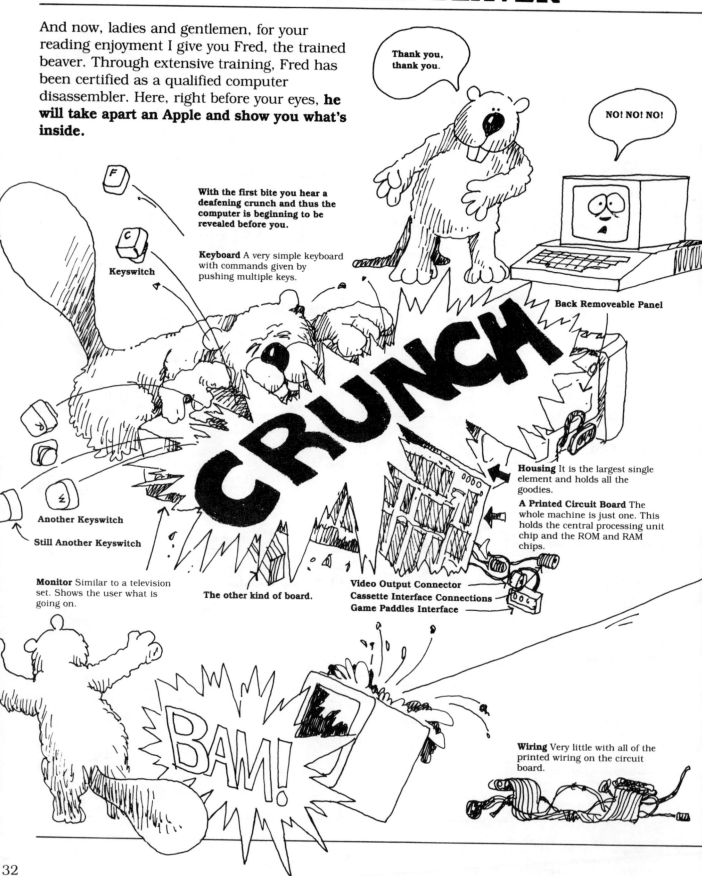

Thank you, thank you.

NO! NO! NO!

With the first bite you hear a deafening crunch and thus the computer is beginning to be revealed before you.

Keyboard A very simple keyboard with commands given by pushing multiple keys.

Keyswitch

Back Removeable Panel

Another Keyswitch

Still Another Keyswitch

Housing It is the largest single element and holds all the goodies.

A Printed Circuit Board The whole machine is just one. This holds the central processing unit chip and the ROM and RAM chips.

Monitor Similar to a television set. Shows the user what is going on.

The other kind of board.

Video Output Connector
Cassette Interface Connections
Game Paddles Interface

Wiring Very little with all of the printed wiring on the circuit board.

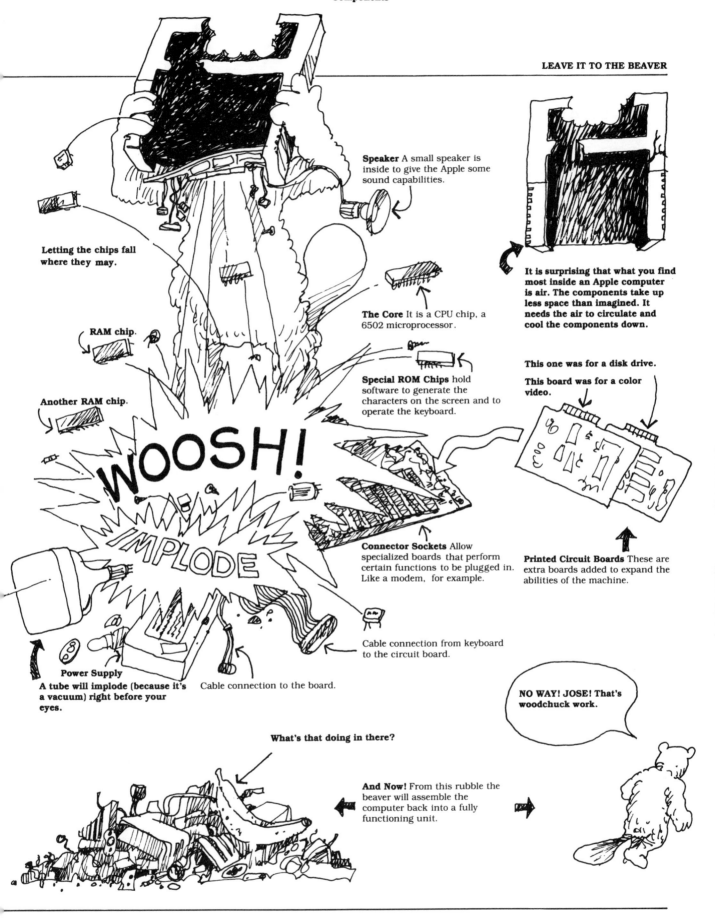

Speaker A small speaker is inside to give the Apple some sound capabilities.

Letting the chips fall where they may.

The Core It is a CPU chip, a 6502 microprocessor.

It is surprising that what you find most inside an Apple computer is air. The components take up less space than imagined. It needs the air to circulate and cool the components down.

RAM chip.

Special ROM Chips hold software to generate the characters on the screen and to operate the keyboard.

This one was for a disk drive.

This board was for a color video.

Another RAM chip.

WOOSH!

IMPLODE

Connector Sockets Allow specialized boards that perform certain functions to be plugged in. Like a modem, for example.

Printed Circuit Boards These are extra boards added to expand the abilities of the machine.

Cable connection from keyboard to the circuit board.

Power Supply
A tube will implode (because it's a vacuum) right before your eyes.

Cable connection to the board.

NO WAY! JOSE! That's woodchuck work.

What's that doing in there?

And Now! From this rubble the beaver will assemble the computer back into a fully functioning unit.

A TRUE STORY

This is the story of one person's struggle to overcome all odds and become literate. It tells the pathos and pain, the sorrow and success of learning to interface with a computer. It tells of the drama when a carbon based brain was trying to comprehend another one made out of silicon. His name was Harvey, its name was Apple, and this is their story:

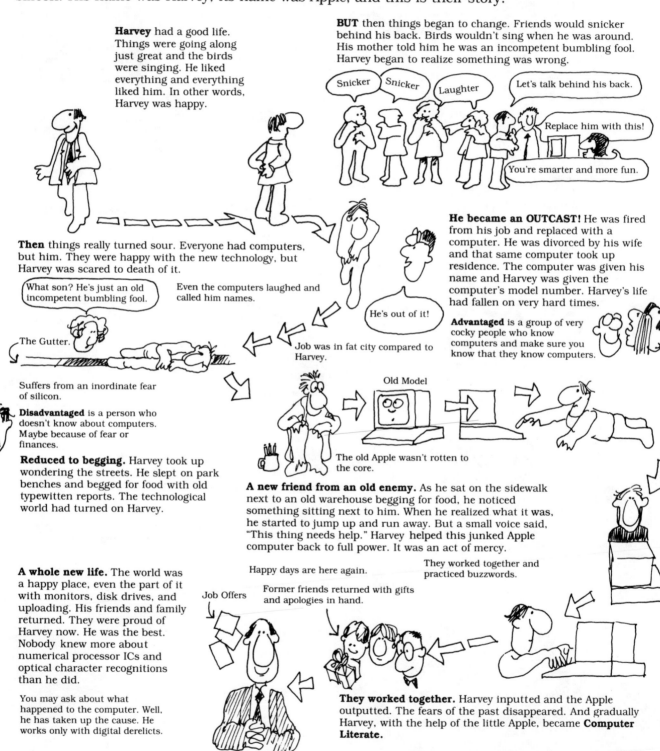

Harvey had a good life. Things were going along just great and the birds were singing. He liked everything and everything liked him. In other words, Harvey was happy.

BUT then things began to change. Friends would snicker behind his back. Birds wouldn't sing when he was around. His mother told him he was an incompetent bumbling fool. Harvey began to realize something was wrong.

Snicker   Snicker   Laughter   Let's talk behind his back.

Replace him with this!

You're smarter and more fun.

Then things really turned sour. Everyone had computers, but him. They were happy with the new technology, but Harvey was scared to death of it.

He became an OUTCAST! He was fired from his job and replaced with a computer. He was divorced by his wife and that same computer took up residence. The computer was given his name and Harvey was given the computer's model number. Harvey's life had fallen on very hard times.

What son? He's just an old incompetent bumbling fool.

Even the computers laughed and called him names.

He's out of it!

Advantaged is a group of very cocky people who know computers and make sure you know that they know computers.

The Gutter.

Job was in fat city compared to Harvey.

Suffers from an inordinate fear of silicon.

Disadvantaged is a person who doesn't know about computers. Maybe because of fear or finances.

Reduced to begging. Harvey took up wondering the streets. He slept on park benches and begged for food with old typewitten reports. The technological world had turned on Harvey.

Old Model

The old Apple wasn't rotten to the core.

A new friend from an old enemy. As he sat on the sidewalk next to an old warehouse begging for food, he noticed something sitting next to him. When he realized what it was, he started to jump up and run away. But a small voice said, "This thing needs help." Harvey helped this junked Apple computer back to full power. It was an act of mercy.

A whole new life. The world was a happy place, even the part of it with monitors, disk drives, and uploading. His friends and family returned. They were proud of Harvey now. He was the best. Nobody knew more about numerical processor ICs and optical character recognitions than he did.

Happy days are here again.

Job Offers

Former friends returned with gifts and apologies in hand.

They worked together and practiced buzzwords.

You may ask about what happened to the computer. Well, he has taken up the cause. He works only with digital derelicts.

They worked together. Harvey inputted and the Apple outputted. The fears of the past disappeared. And gradually Harvey, with the help of the little Apple, became **Computer Literate.**

Computer Literacy Is A CROCK! Why worry about learning more about machines that are increasingly learning more how to deal with you. Computers are getting easier to work with all the time. If you can read this, tie your shoes, or chew gum you can work a computer.

BUT IT SCARES THE HELL OUT OF ME

A Common Fear

In the days of the cavemen, people feared the things of the wild: A woolly mammoth, for instance, or maybe a sabre-tooth tiger.

The fear today is more subtle—but that doesn't make it any less real. The fear most of us share today can be defined in just one word: *computer.*

Oh, the fear may be a little one. It may not intrude itself into our consciousness that often. But it's there just the same. We're afraid of being replaced at work, afraid a computer will dominate us, afraid it will too-drastically change our lives.

Henry's News Story

Henry shared that fear. They had computers in the newsroom where he worked:

"I wasn't about to touch one of those. Ever! I had my trusty old typewriter and that was all I wanted.

"But then one day my typewriter broke down and I couldn't use it. The few typewriters that were left in the newsroom were in use. And I had a deadline coming up. I had no choice. I'd been through the basic training, so I sat myself at one of those fancy word processors and began pecking away.

"At first it was awkward. My brain felt like it was going to go into a freeze. But I kept at it and pretty soon the words began to flow. It was so easy to change words and sentences! I couldn't believe what a helpful tool it was!

"Now I'll never use anything else. I guess you can teach an old dog new tricks."

Just a Tool

It's easy to start thinking the computer is something alive. It's not. **A computer is just a tool.** It was invented to help us out in our lives. It's an extension of the user—and nothing more. If someone doesn't turn it on, it will sit there and draw a blank all day.

A few playful hours on a computer will change most fears.

JUST ANOTHER WHEEL, WRENCH, OR WHOOPIE CUSHION

One of the things that makes man unique (other than laughing at his own jokes) is his talent for making tools to extend his senses and abilities. Other animals can jump farther, fly higher, and lift heavier loads than man. But man can make tools that can do any of these things and do them better. A heavy bulldozer can move more dirt than any bull elephant.

Now a tool appears that threatens mankind's ego. The one area where man holds supremacy over all else is on his shoulders—his brain. The brain gives people a special honored status. But with the creation of the computer, man is threatened.

A computer is not a thing to fear. But not having one when others do may be a geniune thing to get nervous about. Not having a computer and not knowing how to use it may end up putting anyone at a fearful disadvantage. A disadvantage just like not having a gun, or a wrench, or a electrical generator when you need one.

Mankind Traditionally Builds Tools to Extend His Capabilities
The Computer Is Another Tool

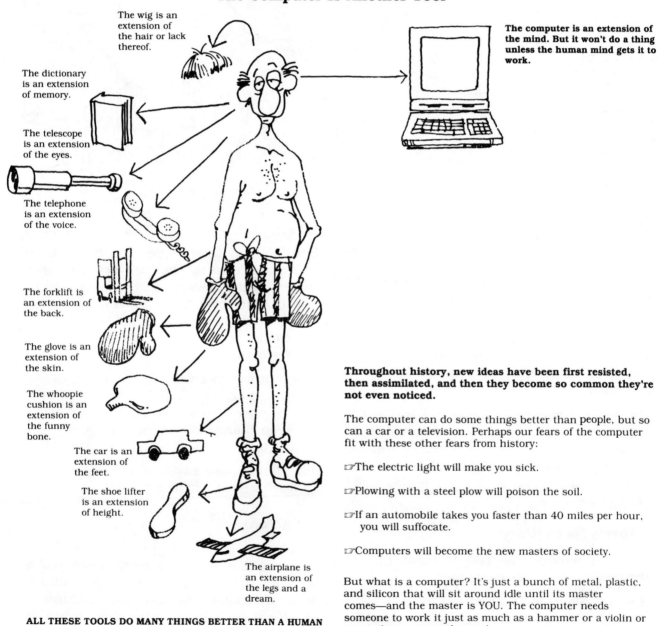

The wig is an extension of the hair or lack thereof.

The dictionary is an extension of memory.

The telescope is an extension of the eyes.

The telephone is an extension of the voice.

The forklift is an extension of the back.

The glove is an extension of the skin.

The whoopie cushion is an extension of the funny bone.

The car is an extension of the feet.

The shoe lifter is an extension of height.

The airplane is an extension of the legs and a dream.

The computer is an extension of the mind. But it won't do a thing unless the human mind gets it to work.

ALL THESE TOOLS DO MANY THINGS BETTER THAN A HUMAN CAN

Throughout history, new ideas have been first resisted, then assimilated, and then they become so common they're not even noticed.

The computer can do some things better than people, but so can a car or a television. Perhaps our fears of the computer fit with these other fears from history:

☞The electric light will make you sick.

☞Plowing with a steel plow will poison the soil.

☞If an automobile takes you faster than 40 miles per hour, you will suffocate.

☞Computers will become the new masters of society.

But what is a computer? It's just a bunch of metal, plastic, and silicon that will sit around idle until its master comes—and the master is YOU. The computer needs someone to work it just as much as a hammer or a violin or an airplane or any other tool.

THE RIGHT CONNECTIONS

Nothing is as frustrating as finding out that the piece of equipment you sunk all your money into won't connect to the next piece of equipment you need.

When one piece of hardware isn't compatible with another, the key giveaway is that the plugs don't match.

Won't work even if you force it.

Doesn't Connect

I think they often make them this way so you'll have to buy only THEIR hardware. If they go out of business or don't make what you need or their costs are much higher than comparable equipment, you're stuck.

The last interface I bought cost me $1000 s!

Connects With Interface

Sure it will fit, but you will have to buy an interface unit. (It says that in very small print.) And because the companies that make the interface units often have the market cornered, they can be costly (an arm and a leg worth).

Connects Right In

Bless them. All you have to do is plug it in, then make sure the software is compatible, and you're in business.

Makes things much easier and cheaper.

Industry standards are finally appearing. If you're buying some hardware **make sure it has certain standard plugs or connections.** You will be very sorry someday if you don't. I didn't and I was.

Other Possible Ports
•Cassette Recorder
•Floppy Disk
•Bar Code Reader

25-pin Connector
Each pin carries a particular signal.

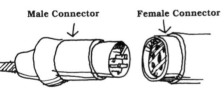

Male Connector   Female Connector

Wonder where they got the idea to call them that?

The critical connection is the **RS-232C**. It is also good to have a parallel port for printers.

Ports The input/output connections that link up the computer to various peripherals such as printers and modems.

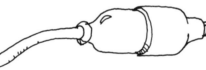
THE BACKSIDE OF A COMPUTER

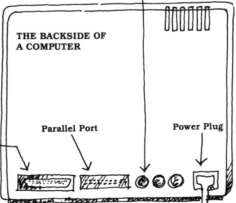
Parallel Port   Power Plug

RS-232C A standard connection to interface peripheral equipment with a computer.

There is a difference between the RS-232 and the RS-232C. The RS-232C is an industry standard with a 25-pin connection and definite signals established in order to operate a modem with a computer.

Plug-compatible You can interchange one device with another. This is usually done without changing the software or hardware.

WHAT KINDS OF STUFF CAN I GET FROM A DATABANK?

If you go to a bank you can get money and if you go to a databank you can get information. There are many different kinds of information available.

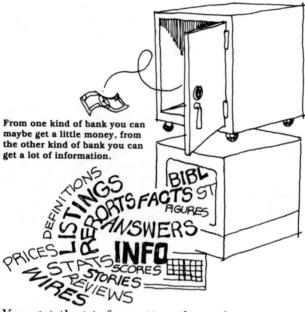

From one kind of bank you can maybe get a little money, from the other kind of bank you can get a lot of information.

You get that information through a computer linked up to a databank. By paying the necessary fees (usually figured on an hourly basis) you can access almost anything that interests you.

A few of the possibilities are:

Available to More and More People

In the past, only the experts could have access to the data banks. Computers and data banks were esoteric and mystical.

But now just about anybody can get into a data bank, as long as they pay the bill. The mystery is vanishing and accessibility and ease of use is taking its place. In the near future it will be as easy as using your telephone.

Some experts haven't realized that what used to be only their domain is now open to the kids.

Send A Note Write someone a note on your computer. Push a couple of buttons, and it's on its way to be stored in the data bank. The receiver opens his mail just by accessing the note which is stored in computer memory on something called the electronic bulletin board.

Leave little Cassie a love note.

Business High demand has made this one of the areas with the most available information. For an example, you can get:

- Dow Jones Industrial Averages
- Company Annual Reports
- Histories of Major Corporations
- Stock Market and Commodities Prices

Find out how the bulls and bears are doing.

Book Information Reading a book on a screen isn't quite like reading one on paper. It lacks the clarity of printed type, but once you get the hang of it, it can be far easier. From these kinds of banks you can get such things as:

- A complete bibliography on almost any topic. I once had it done on a particular subject and I forgot to tell the researcher how much I wanted, so he emptied the whole file. I could hardly lift what I finally got.
- The entire contents of the *Encyclopedia Britannica*
- A partial listing of the holdings of the Library of Congress, with more going on all the time.
- Eventually the actual books of the Library of Congress will be in a data bank.

Medical Information Data banks have listings of thousands of diseases and medicines, with specific data on each. A doctor is only a keystroke away.

It can tell you about that little pill, what it does, and how you should take it.

Turn your head and cough.

Data Base is an organization of data files containing information on a particular subject or a collection of subjects.
Data Bank is where the data bases are stored and accessed.

You and Your Computer can Access the World

Once you learn how to use a data bank, you'll be able to find just about any kind of information you want. With your computer, a door will open to the past, the present, and the future. You can find out what the weeds are called in your back yard and how to get rid of them, or you can study what the stars are made of and how to travel to them.

Sports Wires If you like sports, you can get drowned in statistics of all kinds. NFL, NBA, USFL, WHL, NHL, WBA, PGA, PBA, NL, AL, NCAA, or any other set of initials your heart desires.

Case Studies for Lawyers This can save hundreds of hours of research. McCoy vs Hatfield '57 is what you need to support your case and it's seconds away by computer. You can also use the computer to bill your client for all the research anyway.

Now York Times Information Bank Get a listing of past articles from the *New York Times*, as well as the articles themselves. This can be a great source of information.

United Press International News Wire Get the latest news even before it's broadcast on TV and certainly before it's available in the newspaper.

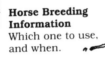

Weather Information Up-to-date weather in all parts of the country. And forecasts, too. But, even if it's from a computer, take an umbrella anyway.

ABSOLUTELY EVERYTHING!

MOST OF WHICH YOU COULD CARE LESS ABOUT!

Horse Breeding Information Which one to use, and when.

Movie Reviews The latest on what's playing.

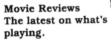

Almanacs Instead of waiting for one each year, you can get an updated version immediately.

Games Entire games can be aquired through a data bank. You don't need to buy those costly game cartridges. *The Alien Mutants meets Snow White and the Magnificient Seven* is yours for the accessing.

Shop at Home A catalog in your computer and and a push of a few buttons sends that *Early American Toilet Seat* to your door.

For More Information

If a data bank sounds like something you want to try, follow these three steps:

GET one of these books. They will tell you what the different banks are and what they have. They should be at large libraries or can be purchased.

Directory of On-Line Data Bases, publisher, Aladra Associates, Santa Monica, California.
Omni On-Line Database Directory, by Mike Edelhart and Owen Davies, publisher, Collier Books.

WRITE to the bases that look interesting and ask for a lising of what they have available. Brochures and other information they send you can be a lot of help.

TRY one of them. Some have no set up charge and rent for a cheap fee. But I had better warn you. This thing can get very habit forming and costly, so take it easy at first.

MAKING A WITHDRAWAL FROM A DATA BANK

Even though there are many kinds of data banks, the steps to borrowing from them are generally the same. (With one exception: most data banks are available to anyone, but access to some professional banks is restricted to members only.) The steps in withdrawing information from a data bank are:

1 Obtain Equipment

Before you can borrow from a data bank, you must have the necessary equipment to work with. You'll need these things:

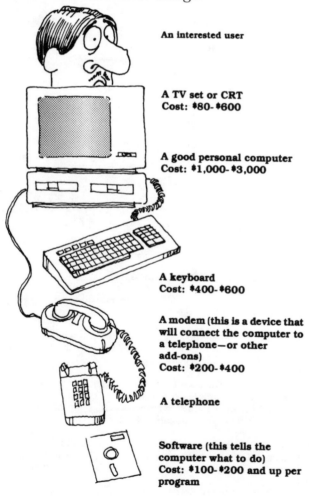

An interested user

A TV set or CRT
Cost: $80-$600

A good personal computer
Cost: $1,000-$3,000

A keyboard
Cost: $400-$600

A modem (this is a device that will connect the computer to a telephone—or other add-ons)
Cost: $200-$400

A telephone

Software (this tells the computer what to do)
Cost: $100-$200 and up per program

2 Set Up Contact With A Data Bank

At first you may feel somewhat awkward in dealing with a data bank. Here's some information that will make the going easier:

☞ Some banks have a set-up charge that ranges up to $100 and even higher. But some have none at all.

☞ Some banks give you free warm-up time to get the hang of things—these are good ones to deal with, especially at first.

☞ Some banks charge by the hour ($3-$5 is average). Others charge a monthly or annual subscription rate that ranges from $50 to thousands of dollars. If you use the bank during their peak hours, they'll charge you more. The prices are lower during odd hours and weekends.

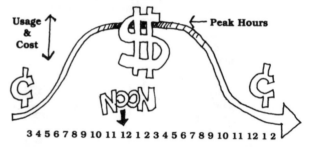

Hours

Lower Use on Odd Hours and Weekends

If you use the bank during odd hours and weekends, you'll save a lot of money.

☞ You can save a lot of time and money if you pick the bank you're interested in and write them. Ask precisely what they have to offer and what their terms are.

☞ Don't forget you may have long-distance charges on the telephone (unless you're in the same city or the bank has a local number or a toll-free number). The peak hour cost is greater here, too.

How to get the money to access a data bank. Make a withdrawal from the other kind of bank. It has always been harder to get money from a bank than information.

3 Call Up and Type in Password

When you become a customer of a data bank, you get you a special access number and password. The combination of the word and number will allow you to get information from the bank.

The more you know about what you want and how to get it, the faster you'll be as you work with the bank—and the more money you'll save.

Don't underestimate the importance of that. You can get drowned in useless information and have to pay through the nose for it. And database buffs like to tell of the man who asked for information on hydraulic rams (pistons) and was given all kinds of helpful ideas on watering sheep!

4 Search, Read, Decide

After you have the requested information on your screen, review it, and decide what you want to keep.

First, transfer it to your own data base—put it into your computer's memory or onto a disk or cassette.

Second, put it into hard copy—run it on your printer—if that's the form you want it in. Don't go straight to hard copy. Wait until you're off the line to the data base.

After you have the requested information on your screen, review it, and decide what you want to keep.

With data banks and the growing use of personal and business computers, some batches of data are being transferred from one memory to another, going from one end of the country to the other, without ever seeing a white sheet of paper.

5 A Few Points to Remember

As you consider data bases, here are three ideas to keep in mind:

☞ Hands-on experience is more valuable than anything else. It will teach you things you won't get anywhere else—not from a personal visit with an expert, not from this book, not from data bank brochures. It may cost you a few bucks, but what you learn will more than make up for the expense.

☞ You can create and rent out your own data base. The more you have that other people want and need, the greater your potential in this area. You can be a subcontractor to an existing bank and get a percentage of the money they get or you can set up your own.

☞ Don't forget the vital importance of knowing just what you want before you start. This can't be stressed enough. Know what you want and how it get it and you'll save yourself 90 percent of the trouble.

Two Examples of Data Banks There are hundreds of data banks around the country. Here are examples of two that are the most popular, try them out to give you a better feel for what data bases are all about:

CompuServe Information Service Box 20212, Columbus, Ohio 43220, toll-free 800-848-8199
One time set up fee is $40 which also gives you five hours. Non-prime time rate is $6 per hour and prime time rate is $12.50. A wide variety of services are offered and publications are furnished to help you find and use them.
The Source 1616 Anderson Road, McLean, Virginia 22102, toll-free 800-336-3366
This one has a $100 subscription rate with a $10 minimum monthly charge. The hourly rates vary from $7 to $20. It offers more than 800 data bases.

The Source is owned by Reader's Digest and CompuServe is owned by H. & R. Block. The big boys are involved.

COMPUTER EVOLUTION

The entire process in the creation and development of computers is one of increasing contrasts. Huge amounts of computing power are ending up in smaller and smaller packages. What used to fill up rooms now will fill up your pocket. It usually costs more to have more of something, but not with computers. With this incredible jump in capability, there has been a corresponding drop in cost.

This computer revolution is now only thirty years old and is just beginning.

1ST GENERATION

Only select professors have one. The first computers were hugh monstrosities that could produce only simple math and a lot of heat, all while they drained the power plant dry.

Vacuum Tube

Little upside-down bottles over very tiny pieces of metal sculpture that ran old television and radio sets.

2ND GENERATION

Only large organization presidents can afford to have one (along with the staff to operate it). This stage is characterized by big companies buying $12,000,000 computers housed in controlled environments to show interested passers-by what the leading-edge looks like.

Transistor

Got rid of the bottles and shrunk a number of them down to a legged metal thimble.

3RD GENERATION

Medium size company presidents can now have one. This is the if-you're-with-it as-a-company stage. Smaller companies could now affort one then spend months of downtime trying to get the blasted thing to work.

Computer Chip

Shrunk a whole bunch of transistors and other electronics down to a thing that looks like a mechanical caterpillar.

4TH GENERATION

Everybody could now have one. It's the age of the personal computer and I'm a person and I want one. What used to be housed downtown at the main office is now on the desk in front of me and the main office doesn't know what to do about it. Not only that, but little Ralphie has one in his room and is now my consultant on numerous technical problems.

VLSI Chip

Packed even more circuitry into a thing that looks like a very small postage stamp commemorating modern art.

5TH GENERATION

November 2, 1992 Just bought a computer; it has the power of a supercomputer and it's the size of this book. It's no big deal to work with. It's much easier to get along with than Sheila ever was.

Possibilities

☞ Denser packing of cheap VLSI chips.
☞ 3-D Chips.
☞ Organic chips of modified living protein.
☞ Crystalline Chips
☞ Modified brain cells
☞ Unknown

Another Evolutionary Step? There are some people who believe that computers are just another step in the evolutionary process. A step that has been greatly accelerated by the conscious manipulation of man. There are still others who feel computers are destined to be our uncomplaining slaves who will take over our work so we can all go fishing. I wholeheartedly support the latter group and will chip in on the gas.

1950 s

Building Size Computers weighed tons, had thousands of tubes, generated a lot of heat and used a small town's power supply.

The Big Ones

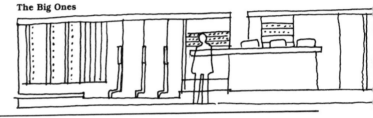

1960 s

Room Size Computers needed special rooms, dedicated power lines, a full support stall and lots of money.

Mainframes

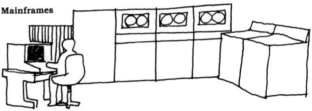

1970 s

Desk Size Computers are office furniture. Users needed special training to operate them.

Minicomputer

1980 s

Desk-Top Size Personal computers that are as easy to use as typewriters, but do much more. Computers become playfriends that don't have to go home for supper.

Microcomputer

1990 s

Disappearing Computers They fuse with so much of our society and our environment that it seems natural to have intelligence in all our technology.

One expert points out that if cars where being developed like computers, you'd be able to buy a Cadillac for under $50, cruise in it at 700 miles-per-hour, and use gas at the rate of only one gallon per 1,000 miles!

Future Computers

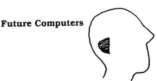

We haven't seen anything until the computer and the biological revolution join forces.

Alvin Toffler

The ideal computer may be one directly wired to the brain. This will be the optimum interfacing. The line between what is computer and what is you will disappear.

The terms microcomputer and minicomputer are so often used interchangeably that they now mean the same thing.

COMPUTERS I'VE KNOWN AND LOVED

Life has been good to me. These girls have shown me a good time and I've learned much from them. They are a little temperamental at times, but with tender loving care and a strong hand things worked out great. Let me introduce them to you:

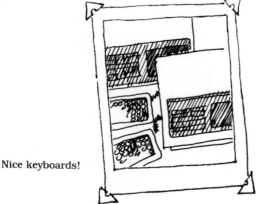

Nice keyboards!

The Televideo Twins These were my first really personal computers. It seems funny, but yes, I started with two. I figured if you're going to go into computers you might as well go double; besides, my partner wanted one, too. These units are very underrated. They are good machines and can compete with the best. But I'm fickle and cheap; I sold them and moved on.

Apple II She was the apple-of-my-eye for a short time. She was a friend's girl, but I played around with her. It was OK though; he gave permission. She had a few silly quirks and they all seem to center on the keyboard and commands. She wanted things only her way, and my friend thought we were seeing too much of each other, so I moved on.

Full of strange little quirks.

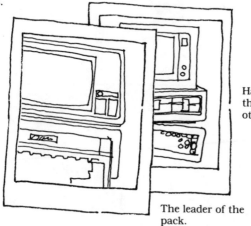

The leader of the pack.

IBM PC When she talks, the other girls listen and pick up on her language. She dominates all the others because of who she is. I seem to be below her station and she gives me only passing output.

She was my introduction to computing.

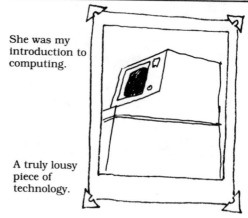

A truly lousy piece of technology.

Big Bertha Her real name shall remain hidden. I don't want anyone to get even the faintest idea of even looking at one of these. She was a real pain. Being temperamental was her continual game. I sold her to someone I didn't like.

She can and will go anywhere.

Radio Shack Model 100 Love her. I honestly love her. She is low on memory and not too quick, but she will go anywhere, no questions asked. Most of this book was done by her.

Looks frail, but she is a real heavyweight.

Has more support than any of the others.

She's easy!

Apple Macintosh We keep having secret meetings at odd hours. We are in tune. She thinks like I think and behind that face is some real brain power. She is starting new daring directions which the others must learn to follow if they want a good user.

That chauvinist! Everybody knows computers are of the male gender.

FILING THINGS AWAY

Just when filing cabinets were taking over all available space on the planet, something new appears. It is called a floppy disk and it's the new better way of storing information. **The difference between the two storage systems are:**

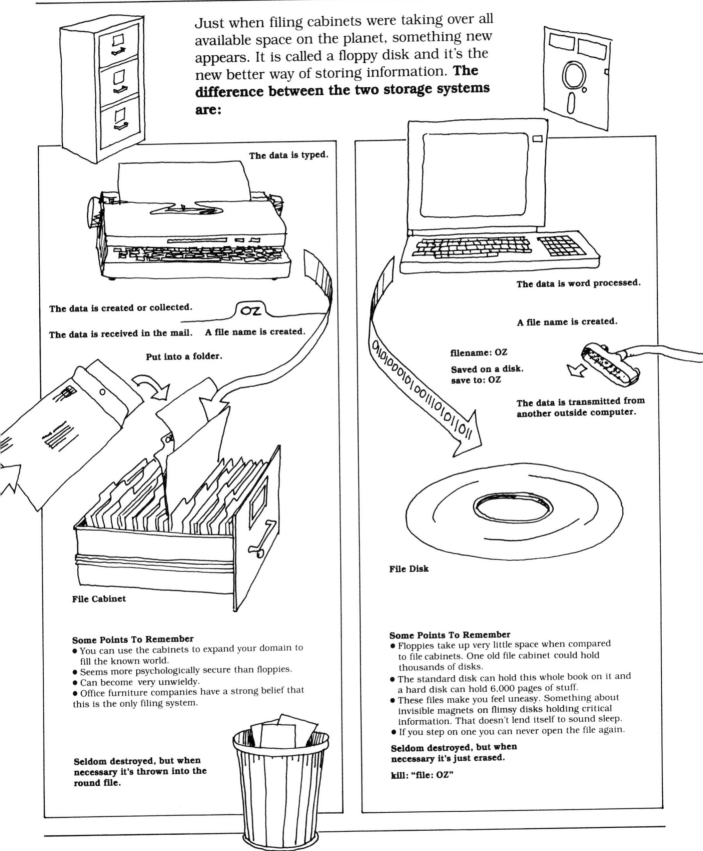

The data is typed.

The data is created or collected.

The data is received in the mail.   A file name is created.

Put into a folder.

File Cabinet

The data is word processed.

A file name is created.

filename: OZ

Saved on a disk.
save to: OZ

The data is transmitted from another outside computer.

File Disk

Some Points To Remember
- You can use the cabinets to expand your domain to fill the known world.
- Seems more psychologically secure than floppies.
- Can become very unwieldy.
- Office furniture companies have a strong belief that this is the only filing system.

Seldom destroyed, but when necessary it's thrown into the round file.

Some Points To Remember
- Floppies take up very little space when compared to file cabinets. One old file cabinet could hold thousands of disks.
- The standard disk can hold this whole book on it and a hard disk can hold 6,000 pages of stuff.
- These files make you feel uneasy. Something about invisible magnets on flimsy disks holding critical information. That doesn't lend itself to sound sleep.
- If you step on one you can never open the file again.

Seldom destroyed, but when necessary it's just erased.

kill: "file: OZ"

WHY FLOPPY DISKS ARE CALLED FLOPPY and some other stuff

Floppy disk drives are the most popular memory storage devices. And since a peanut butter and jelly sandwich that has been flattened under a truck tire doesn't fit well into a disk drive nor store much information, you use things called floppy disks. Here is some information about floppies that you could probably forget:

1 **How To Make Your Own Disks** Now you can have the pride of knowing you can make your own disks.

Find a cassette and unravel the tape.

Pound the tape with a rock into a flat mass.

Cut into a round disk.

This will never work in your computer's disk drive, but only tell people you can make them, not whether they work or not.

8" Floppy Disk

5¼"Floppy Disk

3½"Microdisk

2 **How Much Do They Hold** A 5¼" floppy with 40 tracks holds 125,000 characters. If it's double sided, double that, and if it's an 8" floppy, then triple that. But higher and higher densities are being created continually. The microdisk now holds as much as the standard 5¼" floppy.

Double-sided A floppy disk that has information on both sides of the disk.

Double Density The bit densities between single and double density don't change, just the amount of information that can be inserted is increased.

Magnets They hold the information on the disk. Magnetized spaces record a "1", skipped spaces record a "0".

5 **Why They Are Called Floppy?** It is because the disks are made of a .003-inch-thick, flexible mylar. They are enclosed in a protective sleeve, but if removed they will just flop around.

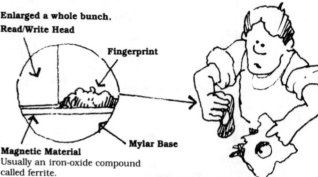

Enlarged a whole bunch.
Read/Write Head
Fingerprint
Mylar Base
Magnetic Material Usually an iron-oxide compound called ferrite.

When you remove a disk from a holder and hold it, you will never be able to use it again. Your fingerprint blocks the head from reading the surface. But it is well worth it to really see why a disk is floppy.

4 **The Common Types You Can Get** The first disks were developed by IBM in 1965 in the 8" format. Later disks were made first into the 5¼" and then into the pocket size 3½" types. The typical size for personal computers is the 5¼" floppy disk, but the 3½" microdisk is rising fast.

3 **How To Cut Up The Pie** On a magnetic disk the data is stored and accessed through divisions called tracks and sectors. These divisions are fenced in magnetically in order to find and file data.

Formatting is putting in the magnetic fences required to put information on the disk. 48 and 96 tracks-per-inch (tpi) are the common densities.

Tracks They are the concentric circular tracks.

Sectors

Tracks

Sectors They are the wedge shaped sections.

Unused	Operating System	Index	Files	Extra Data	Unused	Hole

Section of a disk showing the usual layout of data.

I've seen **disks** spelled this way or **discs** spelled that way. You choose for yourself, but it's probably the wrong spelling.

Soft Sector You have to put in the sectors yourself with software. It's called formatting.
Hard Sector The sectors are put in at the factory. They do it for you.

WHAT MOTHER NEVER TOLD YOU ABOUT FLOPPY DISKS

Be quiet! Don't say anything. Just sit there and listen. And don't tell anyone that I'm telling you this. Floppy disks are inserted into things called disk drives and are read or written on. Yes, believe me. They just take them and open the drive door and shove one of them in. And if it's a double disk unit (hold-on-to-your-seat), they put TWO of them in!

Here is what happens after they're in there:

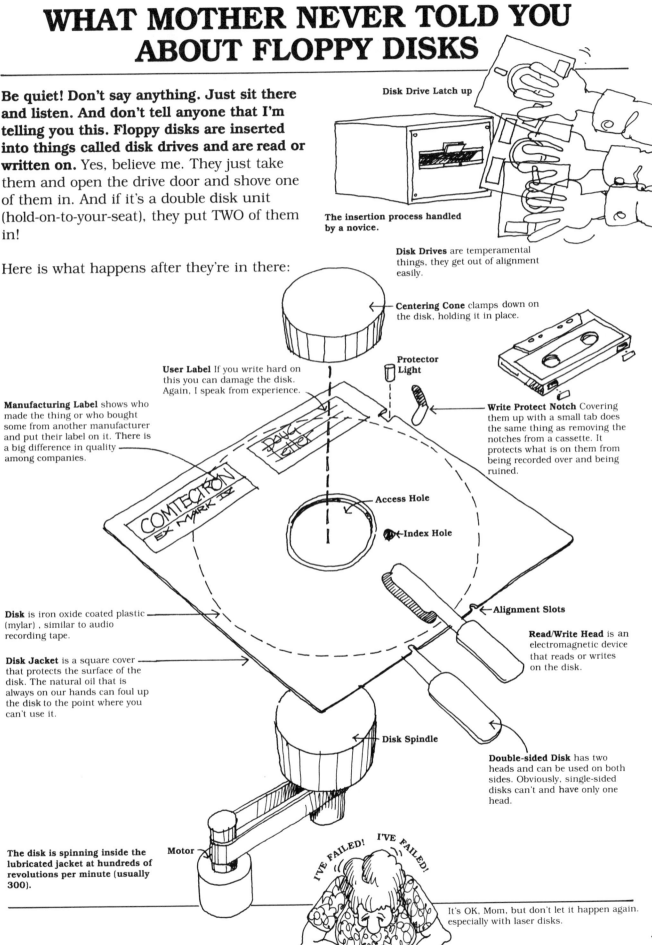

Disk Drive Latch up

The insertion process handled by a novice.

Disk Drives are temperamental things, they get out of alignment easily.

Centering Cone clamps down on the disk, holding it in place.

Protector Light

Write Protect Notch Covering them up with a small tab does the same thing as removing the notches from a cassette. It protects what is on them from being recorded over and being ruined.

User Label If you write hard on this you can damage the disk. Again, I speak from experience.

Manufacturing Label shows who made the thing or who bought some from another manufacturer and put their label on it. There is a big difference in quality among companies.

COMTECTRON EX MARK IV

Access Hole

Index Hole

Alignment Slots

Read/Write Head is an electromagnetic device that reads or writes on the disk.

Disk is iron oxide coated plastic (mylar) , similar to audio recording tape.

Disk Jacket is a square cover that protects the surface of the disk. The natural oil that is always on our hands can foul up the disk to the point where you can't use it.

Disk Spindle

Double-sided Disk has two heads and can be used on both sides. Obviously, single-sided disks can't and have only one head.

Motor

I'VE FAILED! I'VE FAILED!

The disk is spinning inside the lubricated jacket at hundreds of revolutions per minute (usually 300).

It's OK, Mom, but don't let it happen again. especially with laser disks.

GOING WITH THE FLOW

Every computer must follow a set sequence of exactly stated instructions called a program. To create these programs, a visual diagram called a flowchart is often constructed. It shows clearly what needs to be done to solve programming problems.

Computers must have each step spelled out exactly.

Each operation is separated into a step-by-step charting of what the computer must do.

Algorithm A definite step-by-step method to solve problems. After this stage the steps are written into programming language.

A flow chart is a great aid in organizing information.

Turn the book sideways like a calendar and follow the flow.

A dead-end. You've got to flowchart a way back into the flow.

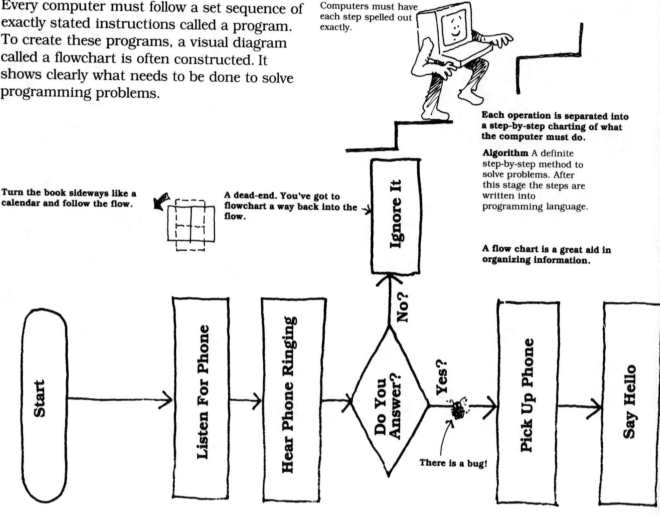

Start → Listen For Phone → Hear Phone Ringing → Do You Answer? — No? → Ignore It

Do You Answer? — Yes? → There is a bug! → Pick Up Phone → Say Hello

Any problem can be broken down into its component parts and each part, in turn, studied and solved.

Flowchart Symbols are standard symbols that represent particular operations. Some common symbols are:

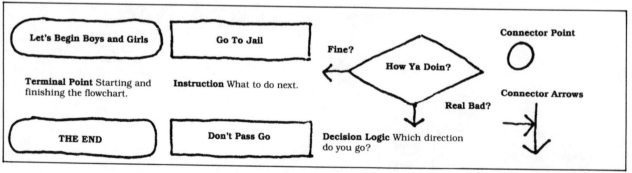

Let's Begin Boys and Girls

Terminal Point Starting and finishing the flowchart.

Go To Jail

Instruction What to do next.

THE END

Don't Pass Go

Fine? — How Ya Doin? — Real Bad?

Decision Logic Which direction do you go?

Connector Point

Connector Arrows

Flow charts are useful to solve many kinds of problems, not just those involving computers.

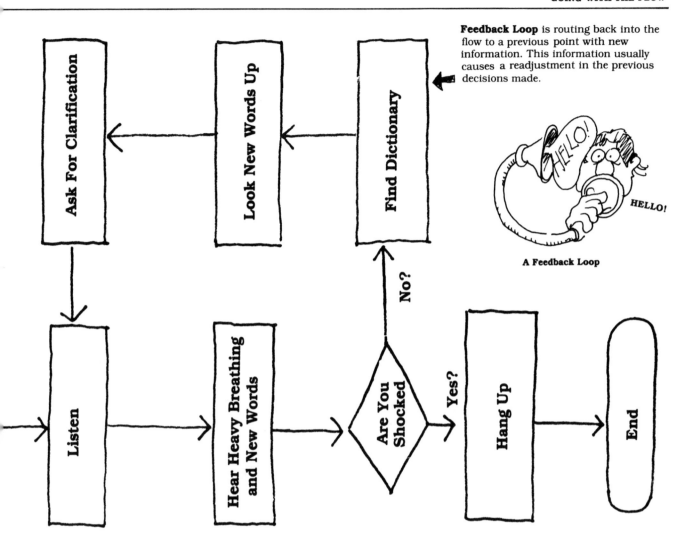

Feedback Loop is routing back into the flow to a previous point with new information. This information usually causes a readjustment in the previous decisions made.

A Feedback Loop

Ask For Clarification

Look New Words Up

Find Dictionary

Listen

Hear Heavy Breathing and New Words

Are You Shocked

No?

Yes?

Hang Up

End

Clearly defined steps help you isolate problem areas.

Turn the book back the way it was before and continue on.

Special Flowchart Symbols are symbols especially made for the frustrations of daily life made worse through programming. Here are a few typical examples:

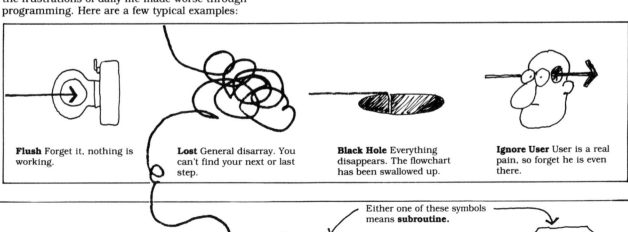

Flush Forget it, nothing is working.

Lost General disarray. You can't find your next or last step.

Black Hole Everything disappears. The flowchart has been swallowed up.

Ignore User User is a real pain, so forget he is even there.

Either one of these symbols means **subroutine**.

ALL-IN-ONE

Right now much of the various media and technology around us is very separate and independent. But the time is coming when it will be possible to combine everything together into one cohesive and comprehensive piece of equipment that does it all. Now the telephone isn't connected to the television, and the newpaper isn't connected to the stereo, and the movie camera isn't part of the newspaper, but they will all someday be interconnected.

A truly personal computer, that becomes an inseparable part of us, involves combining most of our technology into our own portable unit. Sound impossible? Just wait!

First will come the linking together of all the various systems.

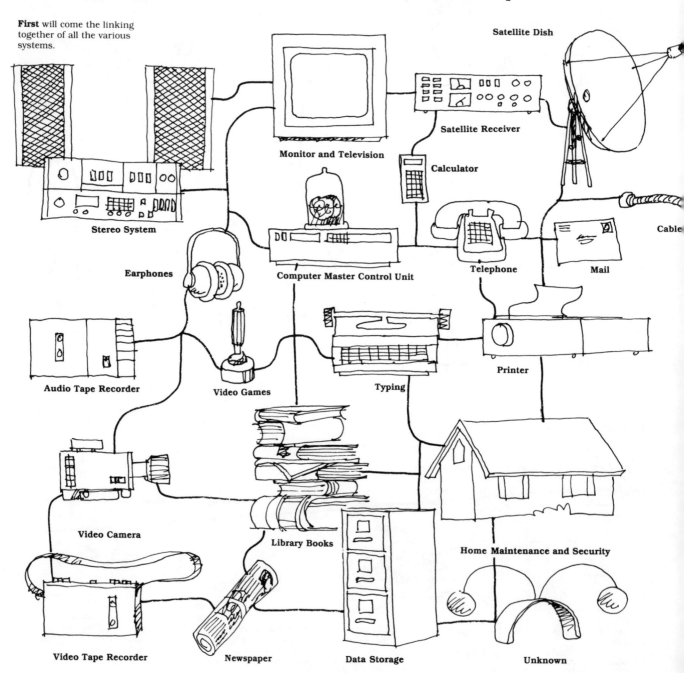

Satellite Dish

Monitor and Television

Satellite Receiver

Calculator

Stereo System

Cable

Earphones

Computer Master Control Unit

Telephone

Mail

Audio Tape Recorder

Video Games

Typing

Printer

Video Camera

Library Books

Home Maintenance and Security

Video Tape Recorder

Newspaper

Data Storage

Unknown

Second they will all fuse and shrink into one system we can easily carry around for our personal use.

The beginning units will look like this:

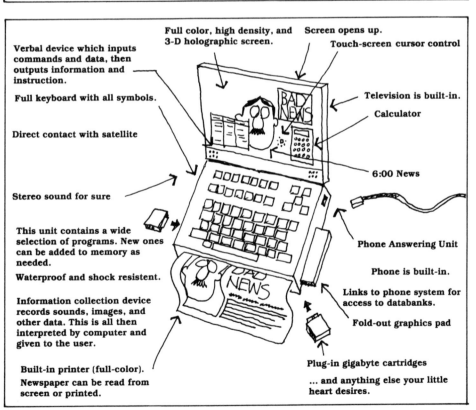

In unique designer colors.

Satellite dish mounted on top.

Television and Monitor are where you can see them.

Loud speaker system and stereo combined

Storage Batteries

Cable link to home, work, and cable TV

Camera

Cable Connections

Control Panel

You name it, we have it.

Loading Zone
• Video Cassette (Beta and VCR)
• Video Disk
• 8-Track Tape
• Audio Cassette
• Reel-to-reel Tape
• Phonograph Record
• Audio Disks
• Bubble Memory Cartridge
• And many others

Support unit is attached (optional).

Printer with extra paper
Newspaper is printed out on command.

I'm sure I will get suckered into buying one of these. Want to buy a quadraphonic sound system or a Beta-format video recorder?

With the necessary refinements and developments, a future computer (total system) could look and function like this:

It does everything—slices, dices, and purees.

Full color, high density, and 3-D holographic screen.

Screen opens up.

Touch-screen cursor control

Verbal device which inputs commands and data, then outputs information and instruction.

Full keyboard with all symbols.

Direct contact with satellite

Television is built-in.

Calculator

6:00 News

Stereo sound for sure

This unit contains a wide selection of programs. New ones can be added to memory as needed.

Waterproof and shock resistent.

Information collection device records sounds, images, and other data. This is all then interpreted by computer and given to the user.

Built-in printer (full-color). Newspaper can be read from screen or printed.

Phone Answering Unit

Phone is built-in.

Links to phone system for access to databanks.

Fold-out graphics pad

Plug-in gigabyte cartridges

... and anything else your little heart desires.

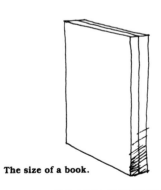

The size of a book.

Part of this complete system is already in place. The entire system is coming into being.

G.I.G.O.*

✱ These initials mean **GARBAGE IN-GARBAGE OUT.** A computer is a very quick idiot. It will work on anything you give it. **Whatever you put into a computer, it will give right back to you.** It will do this very efficiently and on any information no matter how stupid or incorrect it is.

A computer is just a processor of information. It will process garbage just as well as something of value.

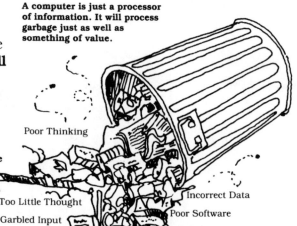

Poor Thinking

If the data is incorrect and the software inferior then ...

Too Little Thought

Garbled Input

Incorrect Data

Poor Software

...YOU GET GARBAGE.

False Expectations

Incorrect Data

Garbled Output

Gobbledegook

False Figures

Fluff

Foggy Thinking

Dumb Ideas

Dashed Hopes

If you put fish bones, empty oil cans and old newspapers into a food processor, then turn it on, you won't have any gourmet meal. You will just have ground up goop made of fish bones, oil cans, and newspapers.

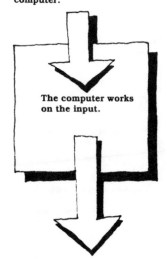

Stuff you put into the computer.

The computer works on the input.

The same stuff comes out of the computer.

There is a belief that computers perform magic. When you purchase a computer, your problems will vanish as soon as it is plugged in.

If you believe a computer will do this without a lot of thinking, frustration and effort, then I'm the tooth fairy.

A computer does not have any values or motivations. It is a complete idiot slave. It will do whatever you tell it to do (if the instructions are correct), and it will work on any data you give it. It will do it without question and comment. It just gives back what it gets.

If you are to get what you want from a computer, then you must **give the right instructions to the right computer to do the right job in the right way.**

Three Heart Rending Computer Stories:

☞News item: Local city finds new computer unacceptable. The computer was purchased for $.5 million to do billing and record keeping. Problems have been frequent and sometimes serious. Experts say it will take another ½ million to correct.

☞"I bought one for the farm. I figured it would keep track of my chicken production, pricing, feed, etc. But there it sits, collecting dust in the corner of the shop."

☞"They got the machine to keep track of the individual projects. It was expensive, but they said it would more than pay for itself in no time. They didn't keep track of the projects before it was purchased. Now they have it, they still don't."

Names withheld to protect the guilty.

WHAT'S HARD AND WHAT'S SOFT?

Computer words are creeping into everyday usage and two words that have done this are the terms **hardware and software.** I heard one of them the other day at the supermarket and then last week I heard the other in a business meeting on advertising. In order to insure their correct usage, please read the following in-depth explanation:

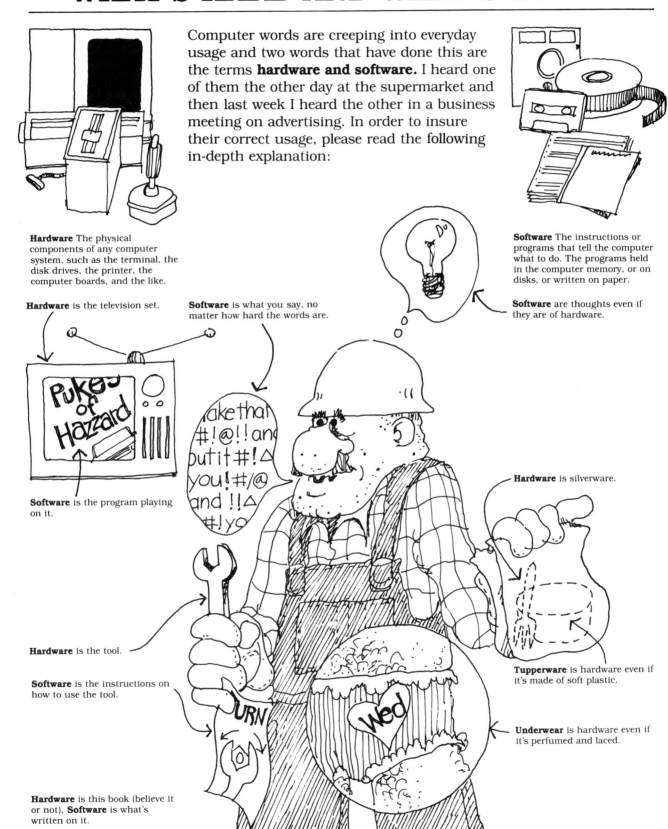

Hardware The physical components of any computer system, such as the terminal, the disk drives, the printer, the computer boards, and the like.

Hardware is the television set.

Software is what you say, no matter how hard the words are.

Software The instructions or programs that tell the computer what to do. The programs held in the computer memory, or on disks, or written on paper.

Software are thoughts even if they are of hardware.

Software is the program playing on it.

Hardware is silverware.

Hardware is the tool.

Software is the instructions on how to use the tool.

Tupperware is hardware even if it's made of soft plastic.

Underwear is hardware even if it's perfumed and laced.

Hardware is this book (believe it or not), **Software** is what's written on it.

Firmware Permanent data or programs that are stored on ROM chips and aren't lost when the power goes off.

THE HISTORY OF COMPUTING

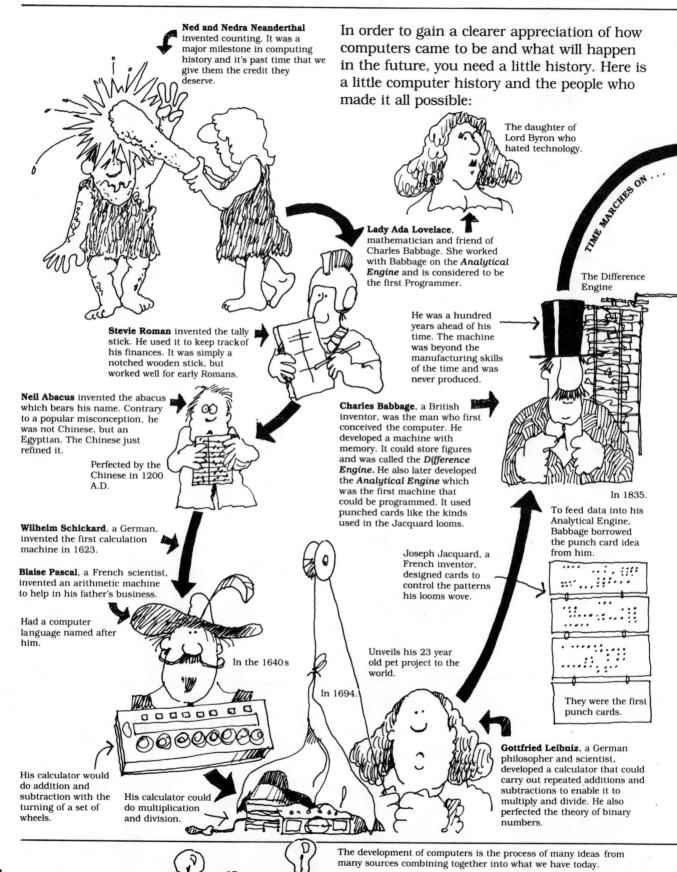

Ned and Nedra Neanderthal invented counting. It was a major milestone in computing history and it's past time that we give them the credit they deserve.

In order to gain a clearer appreciation of how computers came to be and what will happen in the future, you need a little history. Here is a little computer history and the people who made it all possible:

The daughter of Lord Byron who hated technology.

Lady Ada Lovelace, mathematician and friend of Charles Babbage. She worked with Babbage on the *Analytical Engine* and is considered to be the first Programmer.

TIME MARCHES ON . . .

The Difference Engine

Stevie Roman invented the tally stick. He used it to keep track of his finances. It was simply a notched wooden stick, but worked well for early Romans.

He was a hundred years ahead of his time. The machine was beyond the manufacturing skills of the time and was never produced.

Neil Abacus invented the abacus which bears his name. Contrary to a popular misconception, he was not Chinese, but an Egyptian. The Chinese just refined it.

Perfected by the Chinese in 1200 A.D.

Charles Babbage, a British inventor, was the man who first conceived the computer. He developed a machine with memory. It could store figures and was called the *Difference Engine.* He also later developed the *Analytical Engine* which was the first machine that could be programmed. It used punched cards like the kinds used in the Jacquard looms.

In 1835.

To feed data into his Analytical Engine, Babbage borrowed the punch card idea from him.

Wilhelm Schickard, a German, invented the first calculation machine in 1623.

Blaise Pascal, a French scientist, invented an arithmetic machine to help in his father's business.

Had a computer language named after him.

Joseph Jacquard, a French inventor, designed cards to control the patterns his looms wove.

In the 1640s

In 1694.

Unveils his 23 year old pet project to the world.

They were the first punch cards.

His calculator would do addition and subtraction with the turning of a set of wheels.

His calculator could do multiplication and division.

Gottfried Leibniz, a German philosopher and scientist, developed a calculator that could carry out repeated additions and subtractions to enable it to multiply and divide. He also perfected the theory of binary numbers.

The development of computers is the process of many ideas from many sources combining together into what we have today.

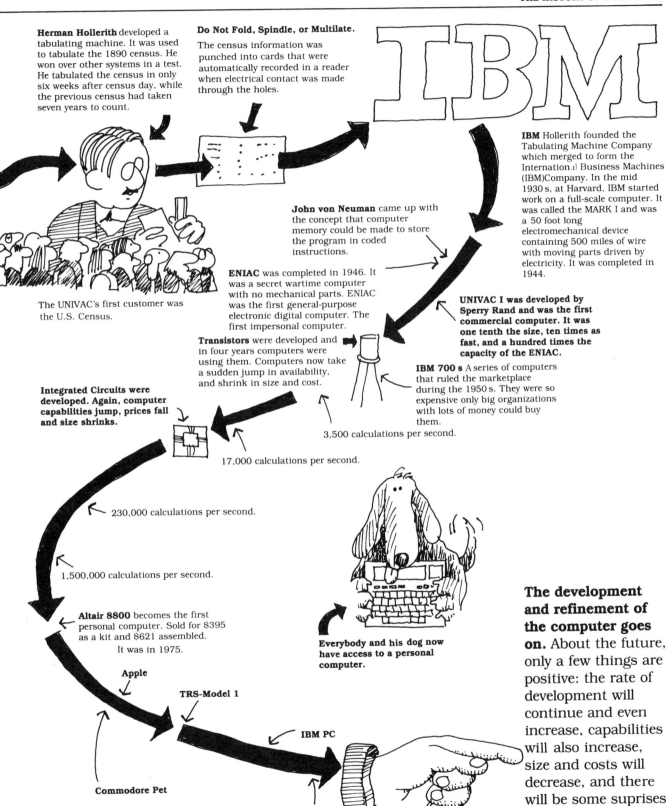

Herman Hollerith developed a tabulating machine. It was used to tabulate the 1890 census. He won over other systems in a test. He tabulated the census in only six weeks after census day, while the previous census had taken seven years to count.

Do Not Fold, Spindle, or Multilate.

The census information was punched into cards that were automatically recorded in a reader when electrical contact was made through the holes.

The UNIVAC's first customer was the U.S. Census.

John von Neuman came up with the concept that computer memory could be made to store the program in coded instructions.

ENIAC was completed in 1946. It was a secret wartime computer with no mechanical parts. ENIAC was the first general-purpose electronic digital computer. The first impersonal computer.

Transistors were developed and in four years computers were using them. Computers now take a sudden jump in availability, and shrink in size and cost.

Integrated Circuits were developed. Again, computer capabilities jump, prices fall and size shrinks.

IBM Hollerith founded the Tabulating Machine Company which merged to form the International Business Machines (IBM)Company. In the mid 1930 s, at Harvard, IBM started work on a full-scale computer. It was called the MARK I and was a 50 foot long electromechanical device containing 500 miles of wire with moving parts driven by electricity. It was completed in 1944.

UNIVAC I was developed by Sperry Rand and was the first commercial computer. It was one tenth the size, ten times as fast, and a hundred times the capacity of the ENIAC.

IBM 700 s A series of computers that ruled the marketplace during the 1950 s. They were so expensive only big organizations with lots of money could buy them.

3,500 calculations per second.

17,000 calculations per second.

230,000 calculations per second.

1,500,000 calculations per second.

Altair 8800 becomes the first personal computer. Sold for $395 as a kit and $621 assembled. It was in 1975.

Apple

TRS-Model 1

Commodore Pet

IBM PC

This Book!

Everybody and his dog now have access to a personal computer.

The development and refinement of the computer goes on. About the future, only a few things are positive: the rate of development will continue and even increase, capabilities will also increase, size and costs will decrease, and there will be some suprises along the way.

UNSUNG COMPUTER HEROES

I felt for years that some of the heroes in the creation and development of the personal computer have been ignored. They were from all walks of life, but all followed the dream of better personal computing and devoted their lives to it. So I've decided to feature their unsung efforts.

Edna Rupture She was the first computer widow. Ralph has been ruled dead by the courts and she has since remarried. Her group **W**oman **H**ungry for **A**ttention from **C**omputer **K**ooks (WHACK) is still growing strong and becoming a major anti-PC force.

Mickey S. Bootstrap The first programmer to make over $50,000 in one year through royalties from his software. His whereabouts is unknown today. He was sent to his room by his mother in 1978 and never came out.

The Silent Ones These are the people who were incarcerated for inserting illegal commands. Let's all work for their release.

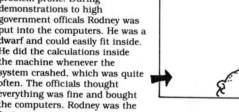

Rodney (squirt) Fuddudler The first computers were very problem prone. During demonstrations to high government officals Rodney was put into the computers. He was a dwarf and could easily fit inside. He did the calculations inside the machine whenever the system crashed, which was quite often. The officials thought everything was fine and bought the computers. Rodney was the first microprocessor.

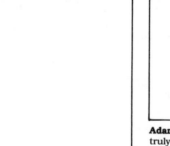

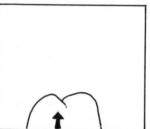

Adam Osborne Created the first truly portable computer. But his business got into financial trouble and it went bankrupt. He lost everything and is now picking up the pieces.

Melvin Mumford He bought the first personal computer. It was an Altair and he bought it in kit form. His purchase started an industry. When I last checked he was still trying to put the thing together.

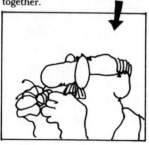

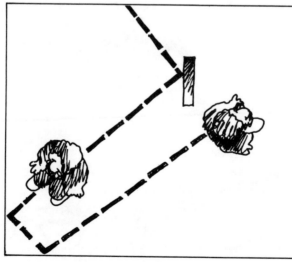

Franklin (Seedy) Seegwick Committed the first computer crime. Tried to steal one of the early IBM 700 computers. He got five years and a hernia for the caper, but he sparked the public's interest in computers.

Noland Bushnell Invented the first video game. It was called pong. He also created Atari. The element of play is never fully acknowledged in creative innovation.

PAYING HOMAGE TO IBM

Once upon a time in fantasy land, the huge giant slept and as he slept the munchkins made music. They worked hard at making the most beautiful music possible. Everybody liked to listen to it. Their little houses constantly vibrated to the music as they created and played it. It was a happy time with each munchkin playing his own creations in his own way. People were always crowding around their homes listening and when the hat was passed around, it came back filled to the top with coins of appreciation.

Then it happened. The giant awoke. He saw the munchkins happy and rich and he too wanted a piece of the action—a big piece. When the giant started to play his fiddle, all the kingdom moved to his music. The music was so loud and so strong the little munchkins had no choice but to play along.

Once upon a time, a similar thing happened with computers. IBM slept (or quietly played with only the big computers) and other littler firms made the little personal computers. These personal computers were objects in great demand. Everybody wanted one for his very own. These little firms made a lot of money and they made it quickly.

But IBM saw all this and decided to get into the act. The big giant started making a personal computer just like the little firms. It was called the IBM PC and it rapidly dominated the entire personal computer market. All the others soon had to dance to IBM's music. This is no fairy tale, just history.

The moral of both these stories is: **When the giant starts to play, all others must hop to his music.**

Runs Their Programs

With their dominance, an ever increasing number of programs are being offered. IBM is even encouraging outside suppliers to create programming. When new programs are created, now more than ever before, they will first be offered in the IBM format.

Knowing all this, it would help to have a computer or related equipment and software that was IBM compatible.

Links To Their Equipment

It helps if the hardware you buy can connect to IBM equipment. That makes possible the interconnection of equipment. If you have already bought some computer that is not compatible, interface units to link-up with IBM are available (but expensive).

Talks Their Language

They use an operating language called MS-DOS. It is an improvement over most previous languages. Compatibles use the same language.

Thinks Their Way

The IBM-PC uses a 16-bit microprocessor (the computer's brain), the 8088 chip. The chip has greater speed, capability, and precision than the 8-bit chip. Other manufacturers have 16-bits that are even better, but they still tend to be IBM compatible.

The day is coming when you can buy a computer and connect it to any other computer, or you can have a program and run it on any machine.

Special Notes:

1. Just because IBM dominates doesn't mean IBM is the best. Other makes are often better. For example, the IBM PC printer is actually an undercover Epson, and the Eagle 1600 (IBM's competition) is considered a superior computer.
2. IBM is an acronym of International Business Machine.
3. Some machines offer a percentage of compatibility such as 99% IBM compatible or 90% IBM compatible. The degree these will work for you depends on whether or not the 1% or 10% missing is just the part you need.
4. IBM didn't pay for this page, but any donation from them will be accepted.

A NEW GAME PLAYED BY DIFFERENT RULES

Our society is in a state of change. We are in a new age. It is the information age.

Have you heard these cliched statements lately? If you haven't, where have you been? Every guru, expert, or man-in-the-street is mouthing these words. They are cliches (I know because that's all I use), but still true. Where in the past these changes took lifetimes, the changes we face today are happening between last night's news-cast and today's. Each of us is having to adjust to change on an almost continual basis. Just when you think you've got it, they go and throw something completely new at you. Our fathers and grandfathers didn't need to change jobs or make education a continual task, but in order to survive—we must.

The Change In Our Work Force

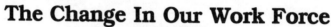

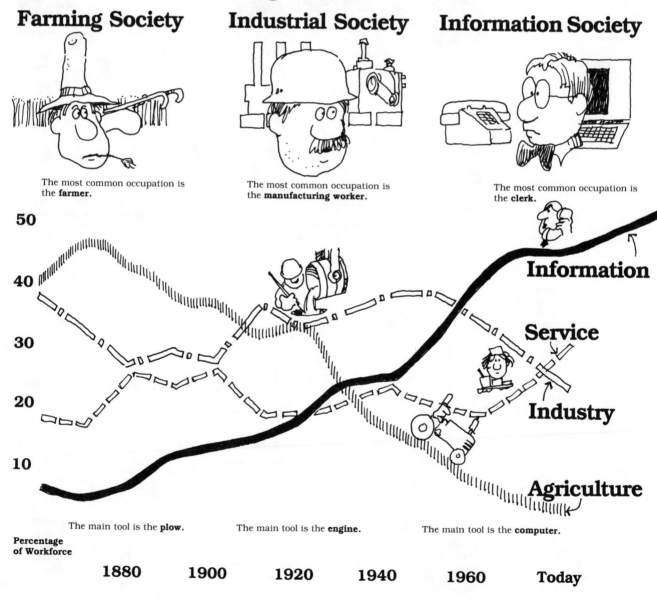

Farming Society

The most common occupation is the **farmer**.

Industrial Society

The most common occupation is the **manufacturing worker**.

Information Society

The most common occupation is the **clerk**.

Information

Service

Industry

Agriculture

50

40

30

20

10

The main tool is the **plow**.　　The main tool is the **engine**.　　The main tool is the **computer**.

Percentage of Workforce

1880　　1900　　1920　　1940　　1960　　Today

This change in society is very real to me. My grandfather was a farmer, my father was a steel worker, and I work with information. Their world isn't mine. I feel the only thing we have in common is our last name.

THE INS AND OUTS OF COMPUTING

INPUT Sending data or commands to the computer's brain (CPU).

Hey, box brain! What have you done to my file? If you've lost it, I'll junk you.

There are two basic parts of any conversation you may have with a computer. First, there is what you say to the machine, **The Input** . Then there is what the computer says to you, **The Output.** The entire conversation of transferring information into and out of the computer's brain (the central processing unit) is called **Input/Output**

Now that you're at the point of saying, "big-deal!", here's more. The devices you do all that putting with are:

OUTPUT Receiving information or instruction from the computer's brain (CPU).

That's an inoperable command. Try again, munch head!

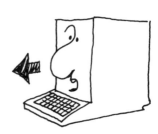

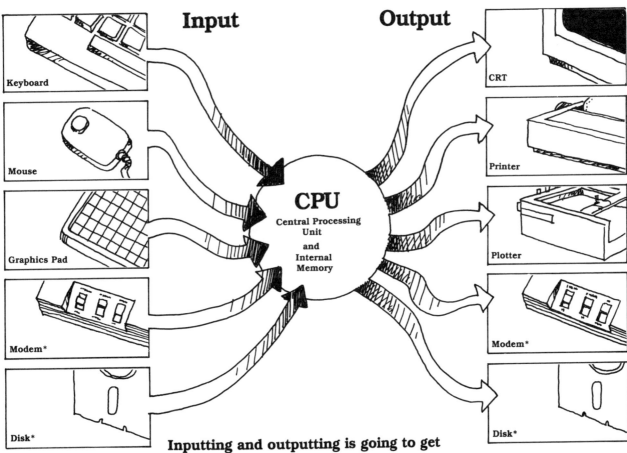

Input   Output

Keyboard

Mouse

Graphics Pad

Modem*

Disk*

CPU
Central Processing Unit
and
Internal Memory

CRT

Printer

Plotter

Modem*

Disk*

* Some things like modems or disks can work either way.

Inputting and outputting is going to get simpler. The easiest way to communicate with a machine is the same way you do it with another human being. You talk to it and it talks to you. You argue, ask questions, and want to see what it's talking about. Technology is heading to that level of communication in computers. Keyboards and mice are second best.

The stuff these devices create, like paper from a printer or a graph from a plotter, is also called **Output.**

I/O An acronym for **I**put/**O**utput.

The most common input device is the keyboard. The most common output device is the television set.

KEYPOINTS ON KEYBOARDS

Keyboards are the most common input device in communicating with computers. It may help you to know a little something about them. So, here is a little something about keyboards:

The brain tiggers a finger to strike a key (sometimes). This generates a code which represents a particular character. For example: the brain thinks A, then the little pinky on the left hand hits the A key, and that generates the character A.

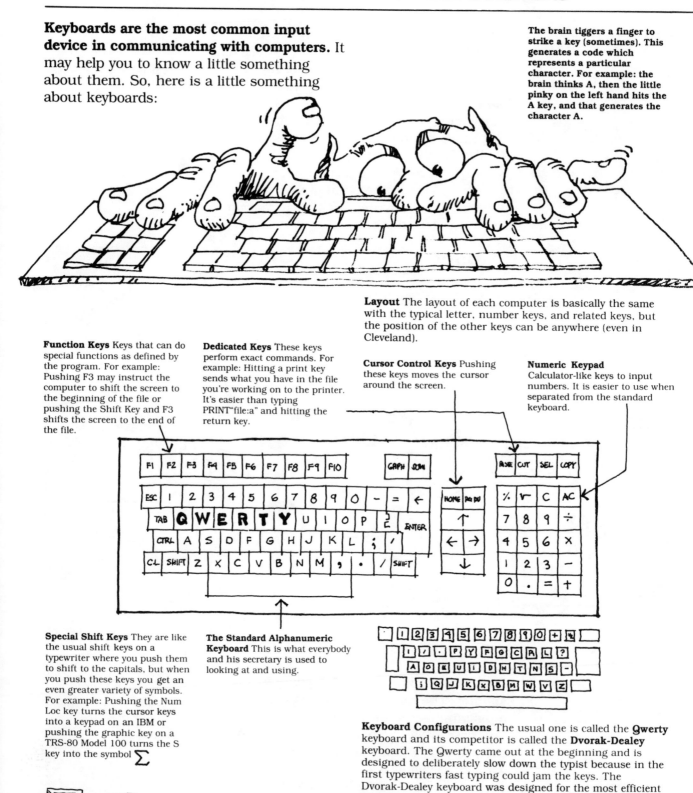

Layout The layout of each computer is basically the same with the typical letter, number keys, and related keys, but the position of the other keys can be anywhere (even in Cleveland).

Function Keys Keys that can do special functions as defined by the program. For example: Pushing F3 may instruct the computer to shift the screen to the beginning of the file or pushing the Shift Key and F3 shifts the screen to the end of the file.

Dedicated Keys These keys perform exact commands. For example: Hitting a print key sends what you have in the file you're working on to the printer. It's easier than typing PRINT"file:a" and hitting the return key.

Cursor Control Keys Pushing these keys moves the cursor around the screen.

Numeric Keypad Calculator-like keys to input numbers. It is easier to use when separated from the standard keyboard.

Special Shift Keys They are like the usual shift keys on a typewriter where you push them to shift to the capitals, but when you push these keys you get an even greater variety of symbols. For example: Pushing the Num Loc key turns the cursor keys into a keypad on an IBM or pushing the graphic key on a TRS-80 Model 100 turns the S key into the symbol Σ

The Standard Alphanumeric Keyboard This is what everybody and his secretary is used to looking at and using.

Keyboard Configurations The usual one is called the **Qwerty** keyboard and its competitor is called the **Dvorak-Dealey** keyboard. The Qwerty came out at the beginning and is designed to deliberately slow down the typist because in the first typewriters fast typing could jam the keys. The Dvorak-Dealey keyboard was designed for the most efficient typing and is superior in layout, but the previous one has familiarity on its side. Keyboards are available on some computers for the Dvorak-Dealey.

Push this key when all else fails.

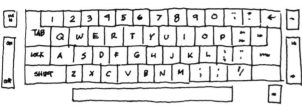

The Standard IBM Selectric (a typewriter) is considered by many to be the keyboard standard. Other keyboards are judged by it as to layout, feel, and speed.

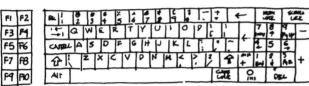

IBM Keyboard Its layout varies from the standard. It has an awkward placement of the RETURN and left-side SHIFT keys. But who are we to question?

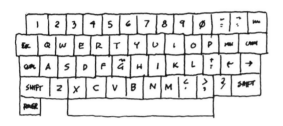

Apple II The keyboard has a typewriter-like keyboard. The various cursor keys and commands are handled by a combination of keys. For example: If you want to load a file from a disk, you hit the CONTROL key and the L key. Some people prefer one small keyboard like this one for doing all the commands with a combination of keys. With me, the more keys the better.

Only one key or button is usually used.

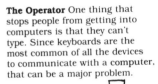

Mouse This input device may eliminate or greatly reduce the use of a keyboard to instruct the computer. A keyboard is best for word processing, but the mouse is best for commands and graphics.

Some Things To Know About Keyboards Here are some points that may widen your extensive knowledge of keyboards. This is one area where you can never learn enough. At least that is what one salesman told me.

Key Switch A single key on a keyboard. A key is a switch with numbers or letters printed on top. Its size and feel is critical in typing.

Connection How the keyboard is fastened to the computer. It can be one piece with the rest of the computer or it can be moveable. With the IBM PC jr., it's not even connected. The more you can move it around, the better.

Membrane Keyboard A keyboard without key switches, but is made into a single sheet of multiple layers. The keyboard is printed on it. When a key is pushed, contact between layers is made and a signal is transmitted. Often used in games, in cheap computers, or in the controls of copy machines.

The Operator One thing that stops people from getting into computers is that they can't type. Since keyboards are the most common of all the devices to communicate with a computer, that can be a major problem.

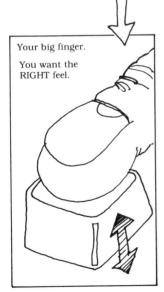

Your big finger.

You want the RIGHT feel.

Can't move this around without moving the whole unit.

The most common.

Uses infrared signals.

The Other Keyboard. →

THE CARE AND KEEPING OF YOUR COMPUTER

Here are a few common sense procedures that, if followed, will keep your computer healthy and happy:

Get rid of excess heat.

Avoid heat from: long runs, direct sun, hot days, heaters, etc.

Keep Between
50°-80°

TEMPERATURE

Heat can severely damage any computer. During operation a computer can build up a lot of heat. Keep the air circulating. Most machines should have a built-in fan or the option of a fan being added. Keep the vent holes clean and open from any obstructions. Keep your computer out of the sun. It can really heat up in direct sunlight. If the room temperature is high that can also cause trouble.

A Surge Protector

Try to give the machine a power circuit with only it connected.

When there is an electrical storm, **PULL THE PLUG.**

Desirable: constant, no change power which exactly meets the computer's power specifications.

$25-$120

Power Surge
From a storm, electrical equipment, or power fluctuations.

CLEAN VIEW

Dust can build up and obscure vision. Remove with a non-abrasive cleaner. Use a clean lint-free cloth or you may be forever looking through scratches.

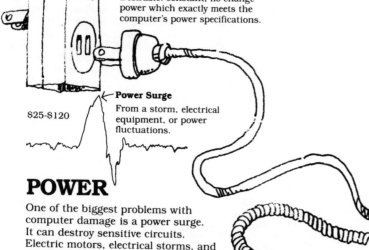

Use a clean, lint-free cloth.

POWER

One of the biggest problems with computer damage is a power surge. It can destroy sensitive circuits. Electric motors, electrical storms, and power fluctuations can cause one. It's worth the protection to purchase a surge protector for your computer.

These static charges can be thousands of volts strong.

Static

Things go better with Coke, except for keyboards.

STATIC

Walking across a carpet that builds up an electrical charge and then touching a computer can send a false code or wipe out something in memory. It is very frustrating when you spend hours working on the computer only to have it fouled up with common static electricty. To prevent this, try raising the humidity and use an antistatic spray or a protective mat on the floor.

ANTI-STATIC SPRAY

WARNING DON'T USE AS A DEODORANT

SPILLS

Spilling stuff in a keyboard can cause erratic behavior of any computer. I once dropped a paper clip in one and it took weeks to find out what made my machine go crazy. Eating over one can be dangerous to it and fattening to you.

DISK DRIVE

Like any tape recorder, the heads in a disk drive can get all gummed up. Use a disk cleaning kit to clean them on a regular basis.

Kits cost $25-$75

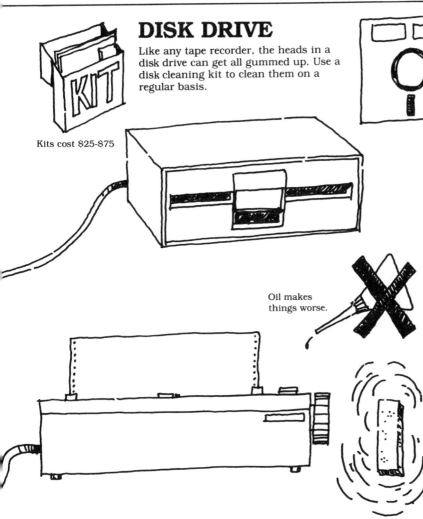

Don't Fold, Spindle, or Multilate

FLOPPY DISKS

They don't function well with peanut butter on them (I speak from personal experience). Avoid touching the disk surface; your hands have a natural oil on them. Dusty and bent disks can't be read correctly.

Oil makes things worse.

PRINTERS

Don't oil them. The bearings are sealed. Oil only clogs up everything. It helps to occasionally turn them upside down and blow the paper fragments and dust out.

ELECTROMAGNETIC FIELDS

A magnet near a disk can garble what's on it. A common problem is getting those magnetic paper clip holders near a floppy. Electric motors, phone bells, and appliances near your computer can cause some very strange behavior. You'll think it's haunted.

AIR QUALITY

The dirt and smoke in the air can creep into the computer and gum it up. Computer equipment can't be made airtight. Clean air keeps the fragile insides clean.

Magnified Many Times

These things eat circuits.

SHOCK

A shock can damage delicate circuits. **One drop and it's in the shop.**

These little creatures (age 3-6) can really put a dent in your computing.

I speak from experience gained in wallet-emptying mistakes. I guess I have to learn from direct experience. I hope you don't.

GREAT MOMENTS IN MEMORY

Throughout mankind's history it has been a never ending struggle to remember. It seems he has always been forgetting things like: what day it is, a birthday, and where the car keys are.

This is the detailed chronology of that struggle:

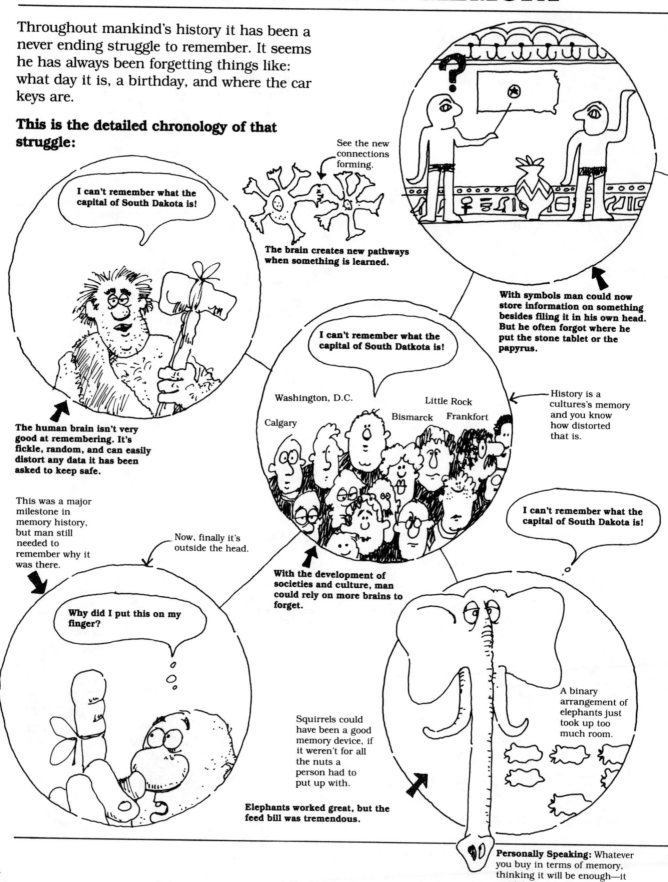

I can't remember what the capital of South Dakota is!

See the new connections forming.

The brain creates new pathways when something is learned.

With symbols man could now store information on something besides filing it in his own head. But he often forgot where he put the stone tablet or the papyrus.

The human brain isn't very good at remembering. It's fickle, random, and can easily distort any data it has been asked to keep safe.

I can't remember what the capital of South Datkota is!

Washington, D.C.   Little Rock
Calgary   Bismarck   Frankfort

History is a cultures's memory and you know how distorted that is.

This was a major milestone in memory history, but man still needed to remember why it was there.

Now, finally it's outside the head.

With the development of societies and culture, man could rely on more brains to forget.

I can't remember what the capital of South Dakota is!

Why did I put this on my finger?

Squirrels could have been a good memory device, if it weren't for all the nuts a person had to put up with.

Elephants worked great, but the feed bill was tremendous.

A binary arrangement of elephants just took up too much room.

Personally Speaking: Whatever you buy in terms of memory, thinking it will be enough—it won't be.

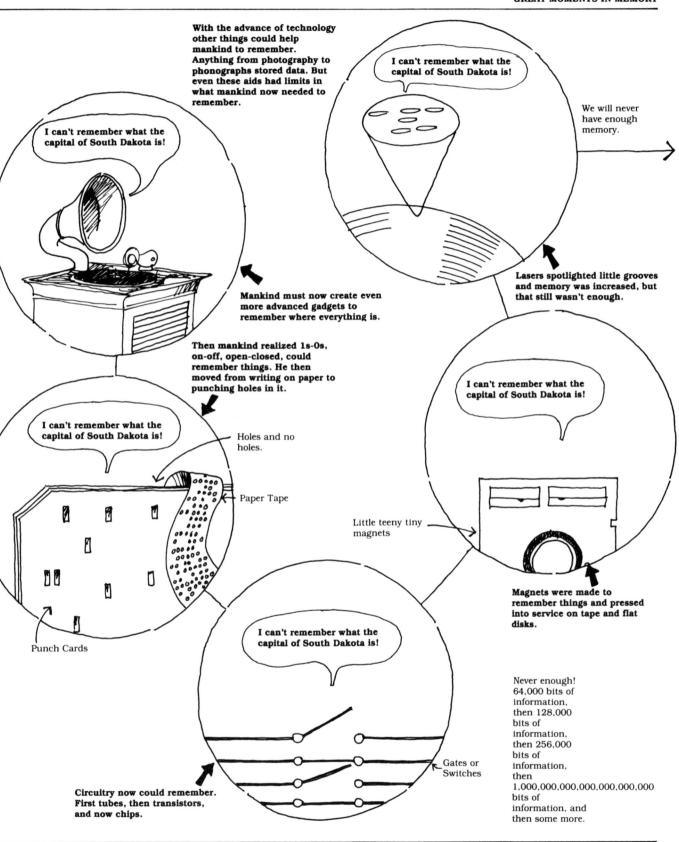

With the advance of technology other things could help mankind to remember. Anything from photography to phonographs stored data. But even these aids had limits in what mankind now needed to remember.

I can't remember what the capital of South Dakota is!

We will never have enough memory.

I can't remember what the capital of South Dakota is!

Mankind must now create even more advanced gadgets to remember where everything is.

Lasers spotlighted little grooves and memory was increased, but that still wasn't enough.

Then mankind realized 1s-0s, on-off, open-closed, could remember things. He then moved from writing on paper to punching holes in it.

I can't remember what the capital of South Dakota is!

Holes and no holes.

Paper Tape

I can't remember what the capital of South Dakota is!

Little teeny tiny magnets

Punch Cards

Magnets were made to remember things and pressed into service on tape and flat disks.

I can't remember what the capital of South Dakota is!

Gates or Switches

Circuitry now could remember. First tubes, then transistors, and now chips.

Never enough! 64,000 bits of information, then 128,000 bits of information, then 256,000 bits of information, then 1,000,000,000,000,000,000,000 bits of information, and then some more.

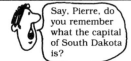

Say, Pierre, do you remember what the capital of South Dakota is?

I dunno.

MAKING YOUR SELECTION

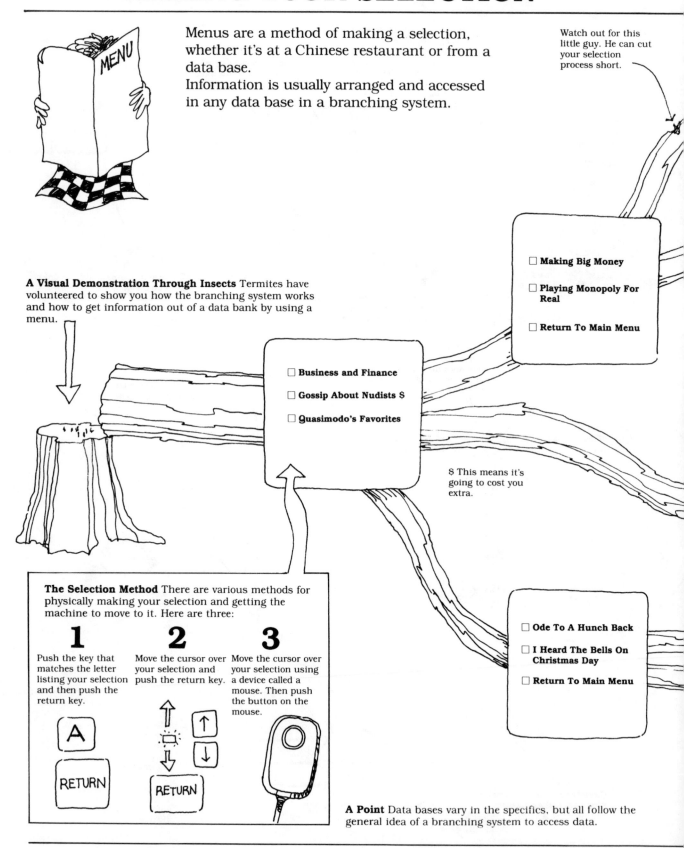

Menus are a method of making a selection, whether it's at a Chinese restaurant or from a data base.
Information is usually arranged and accessed in any data base in a branching system.

Watch out for this little guy. He can cut your selection process short.

□ **Making Big Money**

□ **Playing Monopoly For Real**

□ **Return To Main Menu**

A Visual Demonstration Through Insects Termites have volunteered to show you how the branching system works and how to get information out of a data bank by using a menu.

□ **Business and Finance**

□ **Gossip About Nudists $**

□ **Quasimodo's Favorites**

$ This means it's going to cost you extra.

The Selection Method There are various methods for physically making your selection and getting the machine to move to it. Here are three:

1

Push the key that matches the letter listing your selection and then push the return key.

A

RETURN

2

Move the cursor over your selection and push the return key.

↑
↓

RETURN

3

Move the cursor over your selection using a device called a mouse. Then push the button on the mouse.

□ **Ode To A Hunch Back**

□ **I Heard The Bells On Christmas Day**

□ **Return To Main Menu**

A Point Data bases vary in the specifics, but all follow the general idea of a branching system to access data.

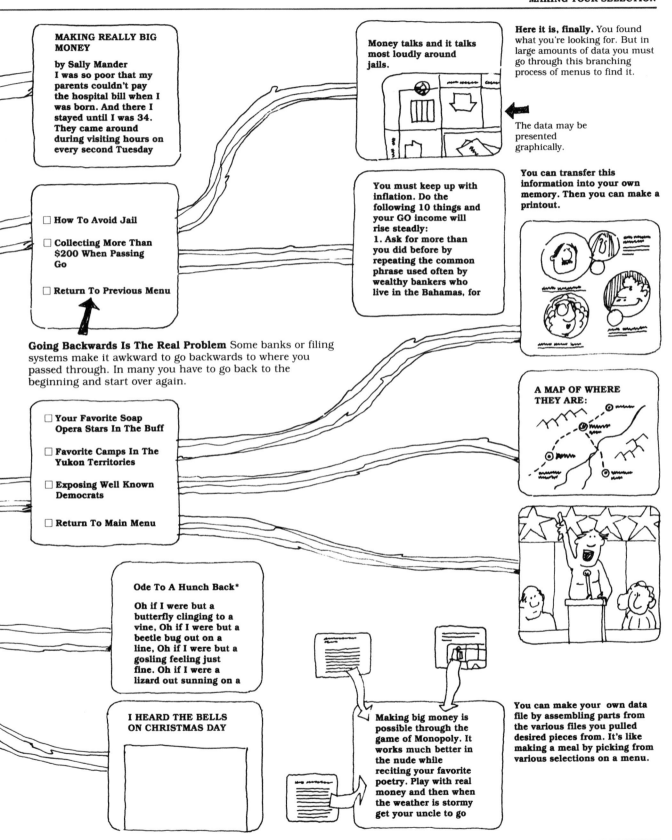

MAKING REALLY BIG MONEY

by Sally Mander
I was so poor that my parents couldn't pay the hospital bill when I was born. And there I stayed until I was 34. They came around during visiting hours on every second Tuesday

---

☐ How To Avoid Jail

☐ Collecting More Than $200 When Passing Go

☐ Return To Previous Menu

Going Backwards Is The Real Problem Some banks or filing systems make it awkward to go backwards to where you passed through. In many you have to go back to the beginning and start over again.

☐ Your Favorite Soap Opera Stars In The Buff

☐ Favorite Camps In The Yukon Territories

☐ Exposing Well Known Democrats

☐ Return To Main Menu

Ode To A Hunch Back*

Oh if I were but a butterfly clinging to a vine, Oh if I were but a beetle bug out on a line, Oh if I were but a gosling feeling just fine. Oh if I were a lizard out sunning on a

---

I HEARD THE BELLS ON CHRISTMAS DAY

Money talks and it talks most loudly around jails.

You must keep up with inflation. Do the following 10 things and your GO income will rise steadily:
1. Ask for more than you did before by repeating the common phrase used often by wealthy bankers who live in the Bahamas, for

---

Making big money is possible through the game of Monopoly. It works much better in the nude while reciting your favorite poetry. Play with real money and then when the weather is stormy get your uncle to go

---

Here it is, finally. You found what you're looking for. But in large amounts of data you must go through this branching process of menus to find it.

The data may be presented graphically.

You can transfer this information into your own memory. Then you can make a printout.

A MAP OF WHERE THEY ARE:

You can make your own data file by assembling parts from the various files you pulled desired pieces from. It's like making a meal by picking from various selections on a menu.

67

WHY ARE COMPUTERS SHRINKING IN SIZE AND PRICE?

Computers started out huge and now they're small. They started out immensely expensive and now they're relatively cheap. What's happened to make the difference? **More and more electronic circuitry is being crammed into less and less space.**

I haven't got the heart to tell him he's being replaced by THAT!

Our generation is going through the throes of a computer and information revolution. As computers get smaller and smaller, they're also going to be able to handle more and more information.

1 The first computers were building-size. They ate up all the power and money they could get to accomplish what a pocket calculator could do today.

2 The next generation could fit into a room. These were the main frame computers. Their capability was greater and they cost less than the previous generation.

3 Then came the mini-computer, the kind of unit that was responsible for our current revolution. This is the computer that brought computing into the office and home. It was the size of a large TV and cost a few thousand dollars.

4 The computer appearing today is the micro computer. Its price is dropping and it's shrinking to the size of this book (CRT & all).

Have you lost your contact?

No, I'm looking for my computer!

5 What does the future hold? Some scientists are speculating that the next generation will be organic computers, with chips modified from living protein. Such chips could hold much more information in much less space. And the chips can even reproduce themselves! But whatever it will be, you can be sure it is going to be a lot faster and smaller.

BIGGER THINGS IN EVER SMALLER PACKAGES

Not too many years ago pocket calculators appeared on the scene for a get-it-while-you-can price of $389.00. Yesterday I walked into a store and glanced at one with many more features for $3.89 (1% of the cost for the first one).

Also, a few years ago I worked with a company that bought a computer system for close to $30,000. Lately, I saw a system doing the same functions with even more capabilities for under $2,500.

From the first computers of building-size to the ones you now hold in your hand, computing power has gone in only one direction. **Increasingly smaller circuitry holds larger amounts of more information.** The cost continues to drop and the computing power increases.*

Vacuum Tubes

Look in the back of any old radio and TV and there they are huddled together in hidding (man has caused another endangered species). The first generation of circuitry was made from them. They were used in the very first computers, which generated so much heat the computers could work for only short periods of time.

They're called vacuum tubes because there's no air inside. The tube is made of glass.

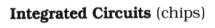

Vacuum tubes were installed on a heavy chassis.

The transistor was developed in the late fifties. It was considerably smaller than the tube.

"**Thanks to these small computers I can have bionic arms.**"

Integrated Circuits (chips)

The third generation was nothing less than revolutionary. Integrated circuits fit entire circuits onto tiny semiconductors. What used to fill up a calculator's insides now is mostly space with a small chip located in the center. So much circuitry can be crammed into a semiconductor that one can be a whole computer.

This chip may have 1,000 s of transistors in it.

VLSIs

The fourth generation is the super chip, the VLSI (very large scale integration). With the VLSI, engineers are able to get more electronics into smaller packages.

The Next Step

Artifical intelligence is coming. Whether we like it or not, machines that think are just around the corner. With the huge computing power coming up, computers will be to the point where they can start to think. They will put the knowledge of top experts within a desktop computer. This is unlike the overgrown calculators of today.

Circuit Boards

The next generation of circuitry was the circuit board. Refined in the late 1950s, these contained many transistors and other components soldered onto boards. It was a great improvement over the vacuum tubes on a heavy chassis.

The **superchip** combines the huge circuitry of previous generations on something the size of a thumbnail.

The last tube holdout in the computer is the terminal screen, CRT, monitor, or TV set. It's now flattening and soon won't even be a tube.

* The rate of putting more and more computing power in smaller and smaller space is increasing.

MODEM-A COMPUTER'S TELEPHONE

How ya doin?

Just because computers can talk to each other doesn't mean the quality of conversation will improve.

Through a telephone, any two or more computers can exchange any information. But to do this, the computers need the right programs and a thing known as a modem. A modem is a device for converting a computer's digital signals into tones to be sent over the phone lines. A modem both sends and receives signals, translating in either direction.

Fine, and You?

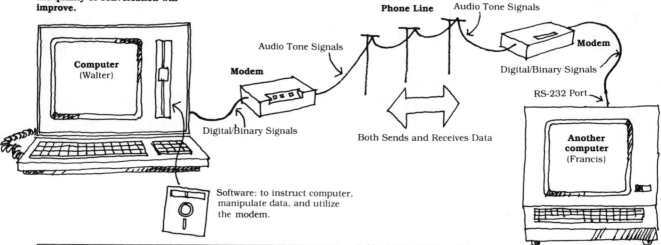

Computer (Walter)

Modem

Audio Tone Signals

Digital/Binary Signals

Software: to instruct computer, manipulate data, and utilize the modem.

Phone Line

Audio Tone Signals

Both Sends and Receives Data

Modem

Digital/Binary Signals

RS-232 Port

Another computer (Francis)

BAUD RATE

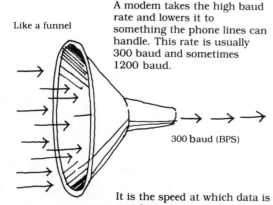

Like a funnel

A modem takes the high baud rate and lowers it to something the phone lines can handle. This rate is usually 300 baud and sometimes 1200 baud.

1,000s of baud

300 baud (BPS)

Baud is the rate of data FLOW.

It is the speed at which data is sent between computers. It is the number of bits of information transmitted per second (BPS).

A good rule-of-thumb is to divide the baud rate by 10 to give the approximate words sent per minute.

Price $100-$600 and up

Software You need a telephone communication program (telecom) to instruct the computer on how to send and receive the data through the modem. The software must be compatible with the hardware.

Phone Lines They can be temperamental. They can destroy or muck-up transmitted data. Always keep a back-up.

Direct Connect The modem and computer are directly connected to the phone wires and don't go through a phone's handset.

Modular Phone Connection

Interference Keep away from strong magnetic fields. Like move the television set a few feet away during tranmission.

Nice Stuff to Have in a Modem Automatic dialing and log-on will set up the connection to the other computer for you. Also, memory in the modem will allow you to work the computer as the modem sends the data.

Bell Compatible Works with the standard Western Electric telephone equipment.

Acoustic Coupler This device allows a modem to connect to a telephone headset. Used if you can't direct connect to a phone like the phones in a motel room.

Rubber cup seal around phone to keep out noise.

TEST #53 What does modem mean?
A. An acronym for **mo**dulator-**dem**odulator.
B. The mating cry of lonely weasel.
C. A 2nd Century Roman Senator
D. A punk rock group

MORE THAN YOU WANT TO KNOW ABOUT MONITORS

A monitor is the device that visually displays text and graphics. It is the most common way to output data. How it works and factors to consider in a monitor are:

How They Work The monitor is a large vacuum tube (the last tube holdout). The screen in front is hit by electrons shot from an electron gun from behind. Where the beams hit the phosphor coating on the screen, the phosphor lights up. The beams' positions and hitting power can be varied and directed into a pattern of points called pixels. The arrangement of pixels can form the letter A or a bar graph.

Resolution The sharpness or quality of image. The greater the number of pixels, the sharper the image.

When a phosphor point (pixel) is goosed from behind by an electron beam, it lights up.

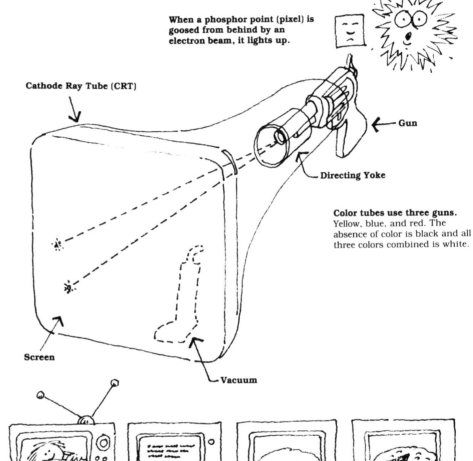

Cathode Ray Tube (CRT)

Gun

Directing Yoke

Screen

Vacuum

Readability The smaller screens have 40 columns of characters, but the better and larger ones have 80 columns of characters. The more the letters and numbers approximate the look of a printed page in quality of type, the easier the screen is to read.

Screen Color The easier to read the better. White on black is the hardest to read. Next, it's black on white. After that it's the green monitor. And the most readable is the amber monitor. If graphics are used, you probably need a color monitor. Color can hold more information.

Color tubes use three guns. Yellow, blue, and red. The absence of color is black and all three colors combined is white.

Refresh Rate The rate at which the image is built onto the screen. If the rate is too slow, the screen flickers.

Speed The speed of the monitor should match the speed of the computer.

Capability The more monitors do and the better they do it, the more costly they will be. The types of monitors are:

Hall Monitor

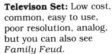

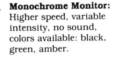

Televison Set: Low cost, common, easy to use, poor resolution, analog, but you can also see *Family Feud*.

Monochrome Monitor: Higher speed, variable intensity, no sound, colors available: black, green, amber.

Color Monitors: Three electron guns, colors and shades possible, number of colors varies, two kinds—composite

video and RGB. RGB produces sharper images; RGB costs more and is digital.

Flat-Panel Displays These displays are now being used in briefcase size computers. The flat screen with its reduction in space requirements is a definite advantage. The kinds are:

- Electroluminescent (EL)
- Liquid Crystal Display (LCDs)
- Electrophoretic Display (EPDs)
- Plasma Display (PDP)

Other than a mother-in-law, a monitor is the best feedback device available.

IF I BUY A COMPUTER WILL IT BE OBSOLETE IN A YEAR?

Computer systems are continually improving at a high speed. Buy a computer today and it most likely will be obsolete in a year. In fact, go look at a computer in the store today, and chances are it's obsolete already!

The question is whether or not you will get stuck with a model T version if you buy a computer.* The answer depends on what the computer is going to do. If a computer will perform an important activity better than what you have now, buy it. If you're buying one not to be left out or to do some nebulous activity, wait. **The determining factor is what the computer will do and how badly you need it done, not the machine in itself.**

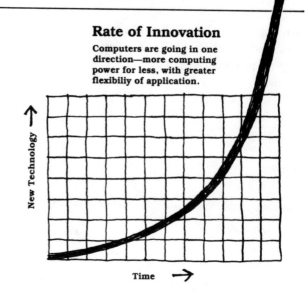

Rate of Innovation

Computers are going in one direction—more computing power for less, with greater flexibiliy of application.

New Technology →

Time →

NEW IMPROVED

♦ **More Memory**
♦ **Injection Phasing**
♦ **Interactive Transfer**
♦ **Ultra-Friendly**

The computer has all the newest features. It is the latest in technology. People are flocking to the store to buy it, but...

CHEAP
Real Cheap

We'll pay you if you take it off our hands.

...will I get stuck with an obsolete computer if I buy it?

When you must travel long distances, even owning a model T is better than walking.

Notes: No matter what you do, someday that computer you bought or are thinking of buying is destined to become a piece of old-fashioned technical junk. You may be able to extend its usefulness a little by making a flower pot or lamp out of it. But eventually the garbage dump is destined to become its home. You can only postpone that day by buying smart in the first place.

A FEW THINGS ABOUT PAPER

I had worked on my computer for days. It was a particularly important project with one of those deadlines that couldn't be changed, no matter what. I could die, but I still had to get it in. In fact, if I didn't meet the deadline I would die.

The project was about finished. Just a few final touches tomorrow morning and the whole pain-in-the-you-know-what job was over and done. I was transferring files from one disk to another. The computer asked me if I was sure I wanted it done, and like any unthinking moron, I said yes and pushed the button. I didn't have the disks in the right slot. There, in a few microseconds, I lost weeks of work and a good Job.

Paper copies backing up a mistake-prone person have been near and dear to me ever since.

A few things about the paper used in printers:

Tractor fed paper is advanced through the printer with a sprocket full of rounded pins that fit into holes on both sides of the paper. This method is more precise in aligning the paper with the type than the friction fed paper method. The paper used is continuous and either on a roll or is fan-folded.

Sprocket

Accordion or Fan Folded

Friction fed paper is advanced through the printer with rollers (similar to a typewriter). The paper used comes in single sheets. This method can be had as an option on many tractor fed printers.

Computer paper is continuous sheets of fan-folded paper. The paper is accordion folded with lines of small holes on either side. The paper is also perforated so it can be separated into individual sheets.

Holes can be removed and sheets separated.

Single Sheets

Paper is an item that is easy to duck, but if you do it can drive you quackers.

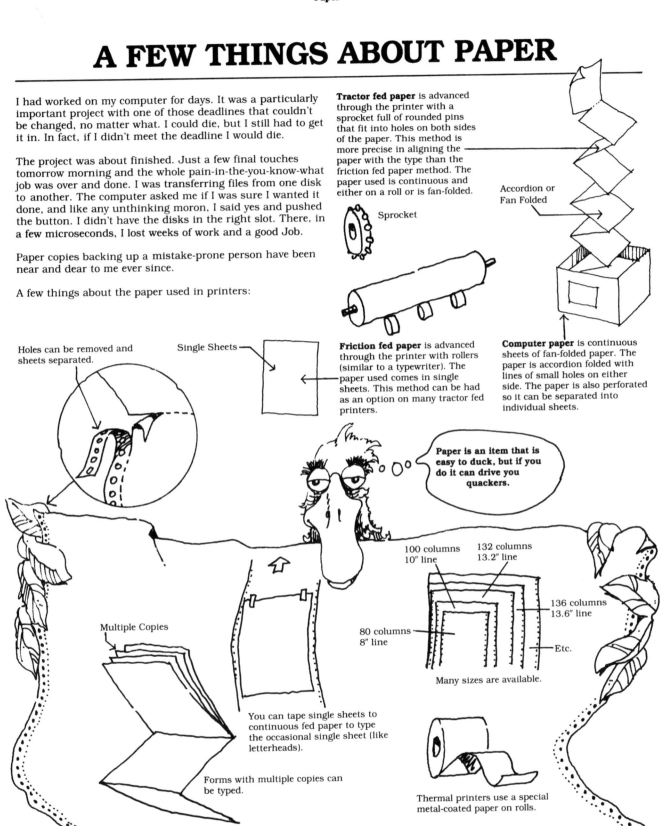

Multiple Copies

You can tape single sheets to continuous fed paper to type the occasional single sheet (like letterheads).

Forms with multiple copies can be typed.

100 columns
10" line

132 columns
13.2" line

136 columns
13.6" line

80 columns
8" line

Etc.

Many sizes are available.

Thermal printers use a special metal-coated paper on rolls.

THE TEST QUESTION FOR TODAY: WHAT IS A PERIPHERAL?

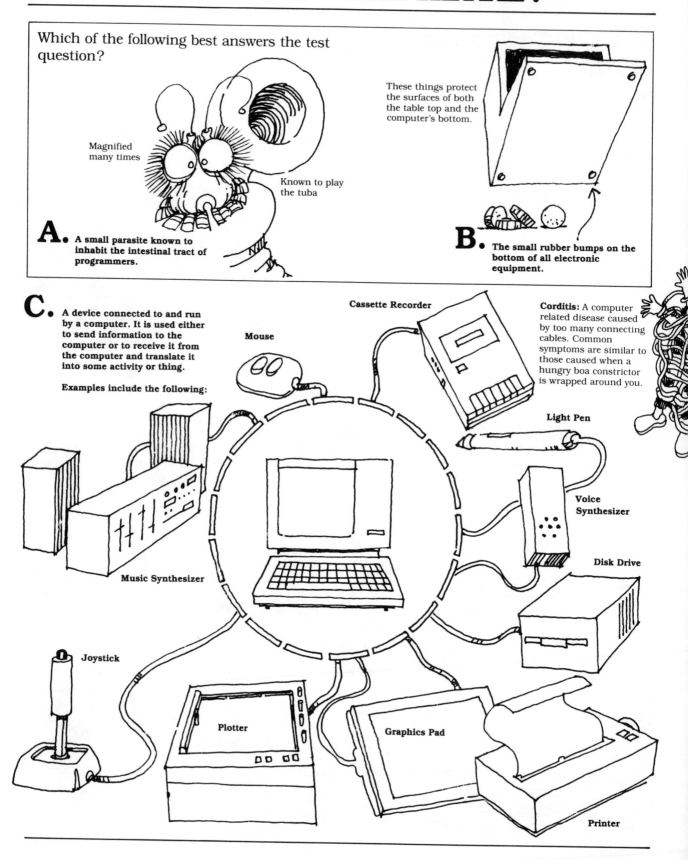

Which of the following best answers the test question?

Magnified many times

Known to play the tuba

A. A small parasite known to inhabit the intestinal tract of programmers.

These things protect the surfaces of both the table top and the computer's bottom.

B. The small rubber bumps on the bottom of all electronic equipment.

C. A device connected to and run by a computer. It is used either to send information to the computer or to receive it from the computer and translate it into some activity or thing.

Examples include the following:

Cassette Recorder

Mouse

Corditis: A computer related disease caused by too many connecting cables. Common symptoms are similar to those caused when a hungry boa constrictor is wrapped around you.

Light Pen

Voice Synthesizer

Disk Drive

Music Synthesizer

Joystick

Plotter

Graphics Pad

Printer

MICE, JOYSTICKS, AND TRACKBALLS

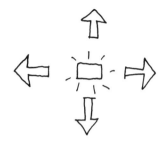

A cursor is not only a user who uses profanity in working with a dumb computer, it also is that little blinking light on the screen. It is used to enter, move, or delete a character. It is also put over a menu listing to select a command. **The cursor can be directed by the following pointing devices:**

Joysticks When you move the stick, the cursor moves in the same direction, but the cursor is probably an alien spacecraft.

Both are used in games.

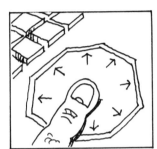

Cursor Disks A round flat area on a keyboard. When you press the disk on a particular side, it directs the cursor in the same direction. Also, the harder you press, the faster the cursor travels.

Cursor Keys Keys on the keyboard that move the cursor around the screen and through the file.

Trackballs Moves the cursor through the various rotations of a ball. It is like an upside-down mouse. Only used in games because it's hard to position things exactly with it.

Cursor Command Keys Make movement easier by moving the cursor to specific points such as the beginning of a file or the bottom of the screen.

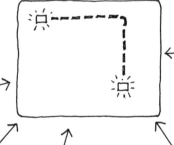

Touchscreen These are the easiest and most obvious devices to use. The cursor moves to where you touch the computer screen with your finger. Used in museums, malls, and libraries.

Touch Pad A flat peripheral device with a touch-sensitive surface. Where you press your finger is where the cursor goes.

Light Pens Same as the touch screen, but you use a pen instead of your finger. It is more accurate with the pen. Some light pens can also work on a tablet. This can be very helpful because your hand often grows tired when touching the screen.

Mouse You put this thing on the table then put your hand over it. Moving it moves the cursor. It has a rolling ball underneath and its movement is interpreted into **cursor postions** on the screen. It is considered by many (including me) to be the best of all the pointing devices.

Digitizer Tablet A flat tablet with a device used to establish individual points in space. It converts linear measurements into digital form. It can also move a cursor to exact coordinates.

Buttons on the top insert various commands.

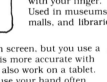

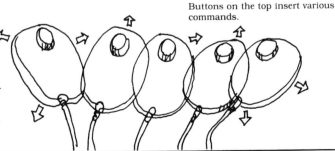

May have separate buttons for separate instructions or one button that can be pushed a number of times to give those same instructions.

The cursor can take different forms: a blinking square, cross-hairs, a space craft, or a monkey. I think a monkey cursor in a business program is long overdue.

WHICH ONE IS YOUR TYPE?

A printer is a piece of electronic equipment for making a typed copy of the data in the computer. This typed material is called a printout or hardcopy.

The reason you buy a printer is to have something produce hard copy in a particular format, at a certain speed, and at a desirable cost. Here are some examples of printouts from the most common types of printers:

The key factors in determining which printer to use are:

Cost They run from many thousands for the high volume units to under $100 for the small thermal printers.

Speed The unit of measurement for speed is C.P.S.(characters per second). A fast machine is over 200cps, a medium speed is 100cps, and a slow unit is below 80cps.

Flexibility You may want both sheet feed and sprocket feed. You may want to have letter quality printing and a faster draft quality printing. You may want to change the type a number of times in a same letter. A good rule of thumb to remember is the greater the range of things you want the unit to do, the greater to cost.

Quality The industry's best quality of print is called *letter quality*. This is usually the type produced from an IBM selectric. All the units copy is judged for quality against this standard.

These units use rolled paper.

The quality is poor, but the cost is low. This may be all you need.

The paper is specially made to imprint without a ribbon.

```
THERMAL PRINTER

This is the story of the aardvark
short story.  One day the aardvar
ant.  "I'm going to eat you," the
his nose up close.

"Beware," said the ant. "I'm a fi

"Great," said the aardvark. "I en
inhaled his supper in one breath.
```

The **Thermal Printer** is a small printer that uses small rolls of special paper. It is an impact printer that doesn't use a ribbon. It creates the copy by applying heat wires to heat-sensitive paper. These kinds of printers are slow, and have a poor quality of type, but they are cheap and usually very portable.

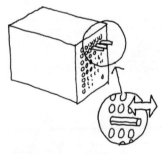

The dots left by the wires hitting the paper form the letters.

Usually there are two matrix densities:

Draft Output

Correspondence Quality

Change the type with a change in instruction from the computer.

The **Dot-Matrix Printer** forms the characters by hitting a ribbon with tiny wires. The more wires it has, the finer the quality of type. This printer has great flexibility, giving the user many type styles and densities, various speeds and can print on different papers. It is the most common type of printer.

```
DOT MATRIX PRINTE
This is the story of the aardvark
It's a very short story. One day
came upon a big, fat, and juicy a
to eat you," the aardvark said, a
his nozzle up close.

"Beware," said the ant. "I'm a fi

"Great," said the aardvark. "I pr
meat anyway!" and he inhaled his
one breath.

This is the story of the aardvark
It's a very short story. One day
```

CPI (characters per inch) measures print size.
CPS (characters per second) measures print speed.
CPL (characters per line) measures density.

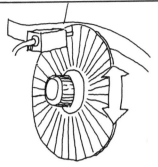

The **Daisy Wheel Printer** uses a unique device for impressing letter-quality characters on paper. It is like a wagon wheel with many spokes, but no outer rim. There is a raised character on the end of each spoke. When these spokes rotate in turn, they are hit by a small hammer. This is a medium priced printer.

The little hammer pushes each character onto the paper as it rotates into place.

To change the type you must stop and change the wheels.

This is the story of the aardvark and the It's a very short story. One day the aard came upon a big, fat, and juicy ant. "I'm to eat you," the aardvark said, and he snu his nozzle up close.

"Beware," said the ant. "I'm a fire ant."

"Great," said the aardvark. "I prefer coc meat anyway!" and he inhaled his supper in one breath.

This is the story of the aardvark and the It's a very short story. One day the aard came upon a big, fat, and juicy ant. "I'm to eat you," the aardvark said, and he sn

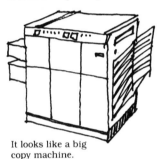

It looks like a big copy machine.

The **Laser Printers** use laser beams to create images on light sensitive drums which produce copies similar to copy machines. They can produce a copy that is superior to letter quality at very fast speeds, but have a huge purchase price.

This unit may set new standards for what it's possible for a printer to do.

This type is better than letter quality printing. It looks almost typeset (the copy in this book has been typeset).

LASER PRINTER

This is the story of the aardvark and the ant. very short story. One day the aardvark came ι big, fat, juicy ant. "I'm going to eat you," the aa: said, and he snuffled his nose up close.

"Beware," said the ant. "I'm a fire ant."

"Great," said the aardvark. "I prefer cooked anyway!" and he inhaled his supper in one breatl

𝕿his is the story of the aar and the ant. 𝕴t is a very story. One day the aardvark

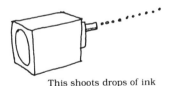

This shoots drops of ink at the paper.

The **Ink Jet Printer** shoots very small drops of ink at the paper. These droplets are directed electrostatically into the various characters. These printers offer quality, are very quiet (unlike the impact printers) and can do color, but there is the problem of cost again.

The type is constructed of a matrix similar to the dot-matrix printer, but of a finer grain.

The drops of ink are magnetically pushed together to form letters.

This is the story of the aardvark a It's a very short story. One day t came upon a big, fat, and juicy ant to eat you," the aardvark said, an his nozzle up close.

"Beware," said the ant. "I'm a fir

"Great," said the aardvark. "I pre meat anyway!" and he inhaled his su one breath.

This is the story of the aardvark and the It's a very short story. One day the aard came upon a big, fat, and juicy ant. "I'm

Laser printer copy from Diser Computers.

WHAT'S A PRINTER?

A printer is a device for producing a printed copy (hard copy) out of a computer. For those of us who are a little insecure with a computer storing all our hard work on something we can't see or touch a printer with its typed copy let's us sleep at night.

If you want to make a printer, here is how. First you saw a typewriter in half, separating the keyboard from the carriage and typing elements. Then you reconnect the keyboard with an electronic brain and place the remaining half two feet away. And finally link the two pieces together with a cable.

The printing part goes here.

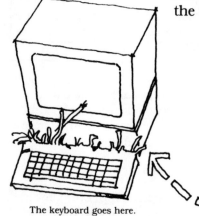

The keyboard goes here.

A Typewriter Run By A Computer.

The computer is directed and the data inputted from the keyboard.

Through a program you instruct the computer what to tell the printer to do and what to say. The computer would seem to be in the way. It is if you type without any errors, never change a thing, or never need another copy; but if you do any of these things, it is a gift from heaven. You can move copy around, correcting and changing things as you go, then when everything is the way you want it, send it to the printer.

The printer is manipulated by the instructions and data you gave the computer.

Kinds of Printers

- Dot-Matrix Printer
- Laser Printer
- Electronic Typewriter
- Thermal Printer
- Electrostatic Printer
- Daisy Wheel Printer
- Ink-jet Printer

Some Factors to Consider When Buying a Printer.

- Quality of type
- Speed of Printing
- Flexibility of Operation
- Cost of Unit
- Portability of Printer
- Amount of Readout Needed
- Amount of Space Available

- Interface with Computer
- Capabilities of Programming
- Future Demands
- Sun Spot Activity
- Quality of Type

- Service Location
- Repair Record
- Paper Specifications
- Paper Costs
- Documentation

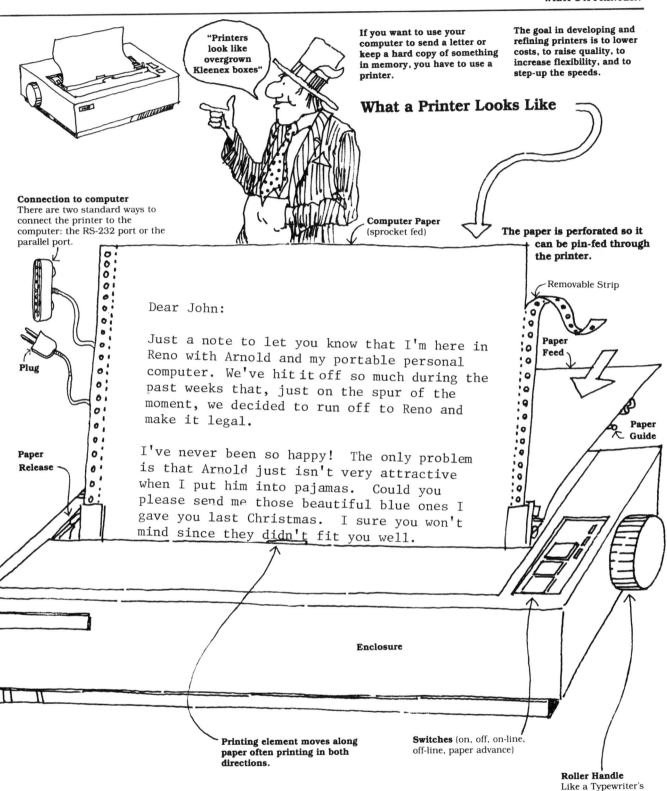

"Printers look like overgrown Kleenex boxes"

If you want to use your computer to send a letter or keep a hard copy of something in memory, you have to use a printer.

The goal in developing and refining printers is to lower costs, to raise quality, to increase flexibility, and to step-up the speeds.

What a Printer Looks Like

Connection to computer
There are two standard ways to connect the printer to the computer: the RS-232 port or the parallel port.

Computer Paper (sprocket fed)

The paper is perforated so it can be pin-fed through the printer.

Removable Strip

Plug

Paper Feed

Dear John:

Just a note to let you know that I'm here in Reno with Arnold and my portable personal computer. We've hit it off so much during the past weeks that, just on the spur of the moment, we decided to run off to Reno and make it legal.

I've never been so happy! The only problem is that Arnold just isn't very attractive when I put him into pajamas. Could you please send me those beautiful blue ones I gave you last Christmas. I sure you won't mind since they didn't fit you well.

Paper Release

Paper Guide

Enclosure

Printing element moves along paper often printing in both directions.

Switches (on, off, on-line, off-line, paper advance)

Roller Handle
Like a Typewriter's

Note: If you get a Dear John from your girlfriend that's been written on a computer, you can answer her through a telephone modem.

HOW DOES A PRINTER PRINT ?

The most common type of printer is the impact printer. It is the kind where a hammer or some other striking device hits a ribbon transferring the image onto the paper. These include the type ball and daisy wheel printers.

Here is how they work:

The tiny hammers used in printers take a variety of forms.

Type Bar This is the impact printer activated by the human computer that started it all. It is becoming obsolete.

Type Ball It looks like a golf ball, but when IBM put it into the selectric it changed typing. It is mounted on a movable axis, moving to the keyed letter and striking the paper all in a blur. The balls are interchangeable.

Daisy Wheel This type of printer offers letter quality typing. It is like a wheel with many spokes, each having a raised letter or number on the end. A hammer hits the end as the letter is rotated into place, striking the paper. The wheels can be interchangeable allowing different type styles to be used even in the same letter.

Dot-Matrix Printer The printing head is a series of very small wires that, when striking the surface, produce dots. These dots can be arranged into varous characters. This allows for great flexibility of characters, sizes, and configurations. The quality doesn't match the daisy wheel, but it's cheaper and more flexible.

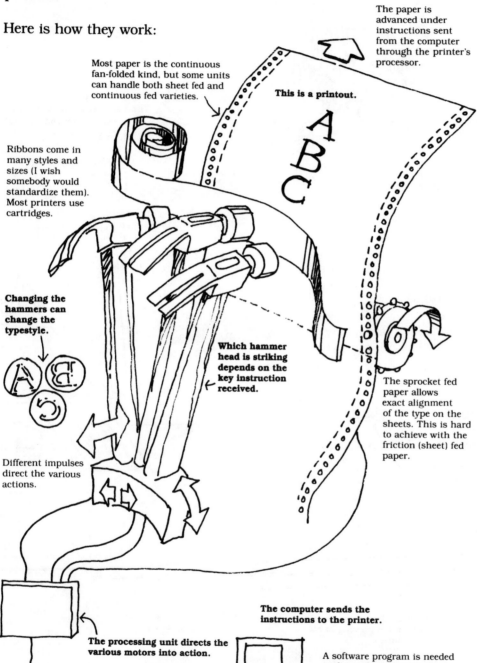

Most paper is the continuous fan-folded kind, but some units can handle both sheet fed and continuous fed varieties.

The paper is advanced under instructions sent from the computer through the printer's processor.

This is a printout.

Ribbons come in many styles and sizes (I wish somebody would standardize them). Most printers use cartridges.

Changing the hammers can change the typestyle.

Which hammer head is striking depends on the key instruction received.

The sprocket fed paper allows exact alignment of the type on the sheets. This is hard to achieve with the friction (sheet) fed paper.

Different impulses direct the various actions.

The processing unit directs the various motors into action.

Computer and monitor

The computer sends the instructions to the printer.

A software program is needed to direct the computer to structure the data and to instruct the printer on what to print.

Helpful Hint #17
Keep a hammer around and be sure your computer knows you have it. If trouble occurs and the computer acts up, just an angry look with hammer in hand is often more than enough. Remember! Fear can be an effective motivational tool on any electronic brain's performance.

TELLING A COMPUTER WHAT TO THINK

If you want a computer to do any task, you must feed it a sequence of instructions called a program. A program turns a piece of technical junk into a thing that can organize and manage information. Once programmed and a computer almost comes alive and can do things ranging from games to filing, and from figure analysis to mass mailings. Here is a typical odd program:

This program has been filed and stored on a disk. There are two because one is a backup in case one is damaged.

A Printout It is the hardcopy (typed sheet) of a computer program.

Programming can be grueling and painstaking work. One step out of place and there's plenty of problems.

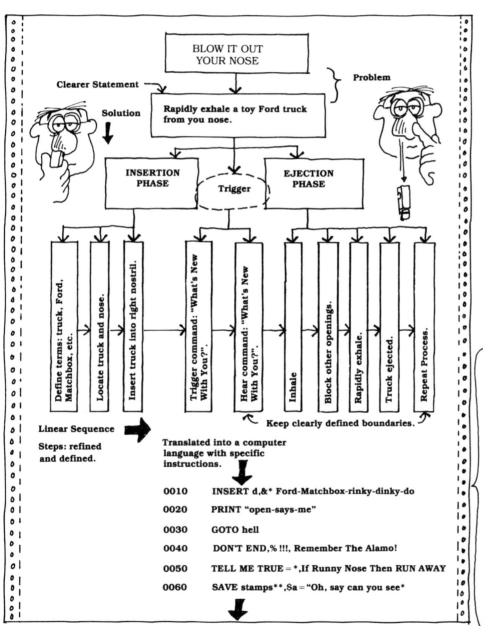

BLOW IT OUT YOUR NOSE

Problem

Clearer Statement

Solution

Rapidly exhale a toy Ford truck from you nose.

INSERTION PHASE — Trigger — EJECTION PHASE

- Define terms: truck, Ford, Matchbox, etc.
- Locate truck and nose.
- Insert truck into right nostril.
- Trigger command: "What's New With You?".
- Hear command: "What's New With You?".
- Inhale
- Block other openings.
- Rapidly exhale.
- Truck ejected.
- Repeat Process.

Keep clearly defined boundaries.

Linear Sequence

Steps: refined and defined.

Translated into a computer language with specific instructions.

```
0010    INSERT d,&* Ford-Matchbox-rinky-dinky-do
0020    PRINT "open-says-me"
0030    GOTO hell
0040    DON'T END,%!!!, Remember The Alamo!
0050    TELL ME TRUE = *,If Runny Nose Then RUN AWAY
0060    SAVE stamps**,$a = "Oh, say can you see*
```

THE BASIC STEPS IN CREATING A COMPUTER PROGRAM ARE:

1. Define exactly what the problem is.
2. Define clearly what the solution should be.
3. Establish the steps that will bring the problem into a solution.
4. Sequence the steps.
5. Write the steps into a computer language.
6. Test run the program.
7. Remove all errors.
8. Run it again.
9. Sell the program.
10. Wait to receive fat royalty checks.

Each word must be stated exactly. You can't INFER anything with a computer.

Like any ordinary language, computer languages come in dialects. This is a strange BASIC dialect used only on rainy nights in Georgia.

Remember Every single character has its meaning. Leave one out and you'll have troubles.

The computer interprets each command and translates it into numbers. The numbers then are translated into a series of electrical signals.

The average commercial program can have over 50,000 separate instructions in it.

81

THE FIELD GUIDE TO PROGRAMMERS

With the coming of computers, another strange creature has suddenly appeared. Its habitat is located right next to the terminals, CRTs, and peripherals. It is a symbiotic relationship between living beings and silicon brains. These computer mutants can be fascinating to observe, especially in their natural environment. The following information can be helpful in understanding and observing them:

These creatures are nocturnal and inhabit the subterranean lairs of computers. These locations are usually in the basement of science and math departments.

The Common Hacker This creature inhabits the never-never-world between man and machine. Here are some distinguishing characteristics to watch for:

Plumage It's long stringy hair. No time for mirrors, or combs. Computers don't care how you look; only how you input.

Sounds They can often be heard uttering a strange binary language. Computers seem to completely understand it, but not the rest of us.

Local Adaptations They're quite flexible creatures and show an incredible variation in plumage, size, and other physical characteristics when adapting to different habitats. See for yourself:

Glasses are typical

T-Shirt and Jacket Through extensive observation, I believe this is actually skin and can't be removed.

MIT

Pocket Clutter I think it contains every pen they ever owned.

Real World A non-hacker world of non-programmers and the location of the status quo.

Stanford

Hands Full They carry around numerous printouts and floppy disks all the time.

Don't ever touch these things if you don't want trouble.

Loners They travel alone. People aren't their thing, but computers are.

UCLA

Jeans They're faded and well worn. They have to be beaten into submission with a stick to get them on.

Kentucky

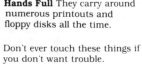

Socks What socks?

Hackerland They live in a world of their own creation. Gods, lords, and masters over a world outsiders can't even imagine.

Sneakers They're tattered and worn. The lace has been broken and retied many times.

Nesting They use computer paper and junk food wrappers to create a rather chaotic nest. Eggs are always laid at programming time.

Mating Dance Since they never mate, there is no reason to dance about it.

Territorial Warning Cry Hackers give off this warning whenever another living person approaches.

Gonk Out They don't sleep, at least not the way most people do. They just cease to function for awhile.

Interesting Types There are a few select varieties that are of particular interest. Here are a few distinctive attributes that will help you in spotting them:

They do a thing called flaming, which is to arrogantly talk incessantly and rapidly about some computer subject they know nothing about.

Pseudo-Hackers These animals are very clever. They act and look like real hackers, but they can be spotted by the trained eye. There are two telltale signs to always look for:

They wear ties and occasionally become computer salesman.

True hackers wouldn't think of doing such things.

Wizard This is a hacker who knows how a certain piece of software or hardware works and can fix it. In the pecking order of hackers, they are at the very top.

Shuffles with an air of quiet confidence

Computer Groupies These creatures follow wizards around and run out for pizza and cokes for them.

Female Hackers They are extremely rare and can only be identified by the longer plumage.

Terminalology The study of the words used by hackers. Here is a partial listing:

Bletch A term of disgust. *"This program is bletcherous!"*

Crufty Something poorly built, or overcomplicated. *"This is standard old crufty DEC software."*

Cuspy Something very good. *"What a cuspy game you've got here."*

DWIM Do what I mean.

DTRT Do the right thing.

Frobnitz An unspecified thing. *Where is my frobnitz?*

Glork A state of surprise. *"Glork, I see what you mean!"*

Grok To understand something. *"Do you Grok that sequence?"*

Greep An overworked hacker. *"On the floor in the corner is the greep."*

Moby Big! *Here's Steve's moby printout."*

Phrog A person whom you don't like. *"That phrog is the department chairman."*

Spazz When something behaves erratically. *"Watch that plotter, it will spazz on you."*

Urglob The strange land where programmers go when they leave the profession. *"He has gone to the land of Urglob."*

The only time they fly south is if there is a job offer or they already live there.

HOW TO GIVE DIRECTIONS
TO THE WORLD'S MOST LITERAL MINDED MYNA BIRD, WHO IN TURN, INSTRUCTS A VERY LARGE AND VERY OBEDIENT WORM

One of the greatest teams around is this bird and this worm. They rate right up there with the other great teams: Abbott and Costello, Anthony and Cleopatra, and Huntley and Brinkley.

These two creatures can be instructed to perform all sorts of activities, but instructions must be constructed in a particular way. Here are the factors to consider when telling what to do and where to go:

The Bird It's a myna bird that has been trained to be first a good listener and then to translate commands into a language the worm can understand and follow. This feathered creature takes every instruction very literally and follows it to the letter. He was trained by the Army.

The Worm It's a very big and very obedient creature. You could talk to the worm directly, but its an extremely slow process. It's much easier to use the bird. Only the bird can translate commands into the worm's strange language fast enough to be worth doing anything. The worm has the intelligence of a typical personal computer.

Unique Quirks There are some very strange reactions you are going to get from these two that you should be prepared for. Here are three examples:

Specialized Instructions When constructing the wording for the instructions, be sure you make every command clear and to the point. This dynamic duo must have everything spelled out exactly. To show you what I mean, here is a test run by a guest programmer. He will move the two from point **A** to point **B**.

Special Note: Before you start telling these two what to do, you must first teach them the meaning of every instruction you're going to give them. For example, what GO means, or what TURN means. Remember, these two are really thick headed.

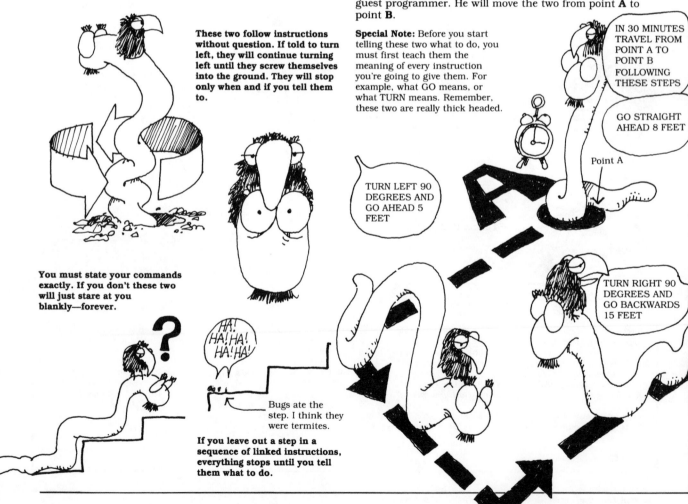

These two follow instructions without question. If told to turn left, they will continue turning left until they screw themselves into the ground. They will stop only when and if you tell them to.

You must state your commands exactly. If you don't these two will just stare at you blankly—forever.

Bugs ate the step. I think they were termites.

If you leave out a step in a sequence of linked instructions, everything stops until you tell them what to do.

IN 30 MINUTES TRAVEL FROM POINT A TO POINT B FOLLOWING THESE STEPS

GO STRAIGHT AHEAD 8 FEET

Point A

TURN LEFT 90 DEGREES AND GO AHEAD 5 FEET

TURN RIGHT 90 DEGREES AND GO BACKWARDS 15 FEET

HA! HA!HA! HA!HA!

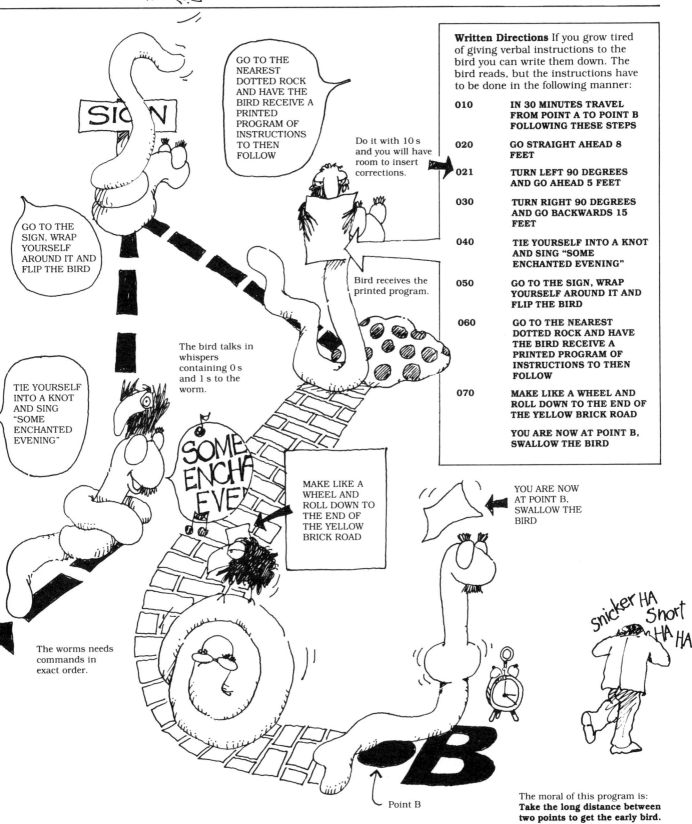

GO TO THE NEAREST DOTTED ROCK AND HAVE THE BIRD RECEIVE A PRINTED PROGRAM OF INSTRUCTIONS TO THEN FOLLOW

Do it with 10 s and you will have room to insert corrections.

GO TO THE SIGN, WRAP YOURSELF AROUND IT AND FLIP THE BIRD

Bird receives the printed program.

The bird talks in whispers containing 0 s and 1 s to the worm.

TIE YOURSELF INTO A KNOT AND SING "SOME ENCHANTED EVENING"

MAKE LIKE A WHEEL AND ROLL DOWN TO THE END OF THE YELLOW BRICK ROAD

YOU ARE NOW AT POINT B, SWALLOW THE BIRD

The worms needs commands in exact order.

Point B

snicker HA Snort HA HA!

Written Directions If you grow tired of giving verbal instructions to the bird you can write them down. The bird reads, but the instructions have to be done in the following manner:

010	IN 30 MINUTES TRAVEL FROM POINT A TO POINT B FOLLOWING THESE STEPS
020	GO STRAIGHT AHEAD 8 FEET
021	TURN LEFT 90 DEGREES AND GO AHEAD 5 FEET
030	TURN RIGHT 90 DEGREES AND GO BACKWARDS 15 FEET
040	TIE YOURSELF INTO A KNOT AND SING "SOME ENCHANTED EVENING"
050	GO TO THE SIGN, WRAP YOURSELF AROUND IT AND FLIP THE BIRD
060	GO TO THE NEAREST DOTTED ROCK AND HAVE THE BIRD RECEIVE A PRINTED PROGRAM OF INSTRUCTIONS TO THEN FOLLOW
070	MAKE LIKE A WHEEL AND ROLL DOWN TO THE END OF THE YELLOW BRICK ROAD
	YOU ARE NOW AT POINT B, SWALLOW THE BIRD

The moral of this program is:
Take the long distance between two points to get the early bird.

BUY FROM A SURVIVOR!

There is a war now going on. It's not with tanks and airplanes, but with computer chips and disk drives. It isn't being fought over land and political control, but over profits and market share.

The Computer War

The rate of new products and price cuts increases.

Everybody brings out new products and cuts prices.
"If they can, anybody can."

People see the money being made and everybody gets into the act.
"If they can, we can."

One or two people start companies to capitalize on those ideas.
"There are mega-bucks to be made with a personal computer."

Starts with the innovative ideas of a select few.

"I've got it! We could put it all on a piece of silicon."

Pricing
WAR!

Shakeout

CRASH

The war drains many of their financial life blood.
"We've got to get the model 2000 out by Thursday and cut the price to the bone."

Many die, a few survive.
"Bankruptcy is our only choice."

Many get into the fight. Few make it.

The suvivors can dominate the industry by being so big they can make things cheaper and sell them faster or they have found such a unique niche, few can compete.

"These prices have to come up."

That new computer could be the Desoto or Nash of tomorrow. There is going to be a filtering out of computer companies. Every other high-demand product has gone through the same kind of war and computers are no exception.

Software companies are not exempt from this kind of war.

This war does affect you. You could end up bleeding in the wallet. If you're buying any computer hardware or software, you could get stuck with something from a dead company. And future products, service, and improvements are hard to get from a dead company. So, if you are thinking of buying something **it will pay to buy from a survivor.**

86

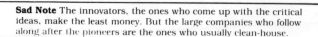

Sad Note The innovators, the ones who come up with the critical ideas, make the least money. But the large companies who follow along after the pioneers are the ones who usually clean-house.

BEWARE OF THIS MAN!

When buying a computer and related stuff, a few simple points about a certain personality (or lack thereof) can save you an incredible amount of money and trouble. Here are the **seven danger signals of a sleazy computer salesman:**

1
Uses the words, "my friend, I've got just what you need."

2
Dresses like he is impersonating a Christmas tree.

3
Sells cars, furniture, or sports equipment with the same approach.

4
Treats you like you were very lucky to be able to dress yourself this morning.

5
Pushes people only toward the materials they will need a second mortgage to purchase.

6
Spouts jargon as if he knows what he's talking about.

7
Talks, but never listens.

I went with a friend to a computer store to help him pick up some software. I had some experience with what he wanted and had a pretty good idea what would work for him.

The salesman took aim at us as soon as we strolled through the door. He looked like a vulture after a long fast. Those cliched words, "Can I help you?" soon echoed around the showroom. We replied with the usual words. "Just looking." Then we made the mistake of casually mentioning what we were looking for.

What followed was a canned presentation to buy the Cadillac of programs. Of course, it was only $660 and a steal at that. I mentioned a key function that it needed, but didn't have. The salesman shrugged that off as being unimportant (I knew it was critical).

We then went to another store, after some trouble in removing the previous salesman from our necks. You can't believe the difference. This salesman actually listened. From his questions you knew he knew what he was talking about.

After a while he raised his finger and said, "I've got a program in the basement that will do the job." A few minutes later, he appeared with a program for $35. It solved our problem.

Can't be hard to guess which salesman I'm going back to.

The last salesman is a rare bird. Not impossible to find, but still very hard. The key indicator in finding one is the fact that **they listen.**

It helps a lot to know one of these. A computer is just the beginning. Afterward, you're going to need additional equipment, software, and, most important, knowledge. **You need a knowledgeable person who is more interested in hand-holding than wallet-lifting.**

Last time I talked to my friend, he couldn't believe how well the $35 software was working.

ANSWERING THESE THREE QUESTIONS CAN SAVE YOU TIME AND MONEY

A little thought before you finally buy a computer can save you headaches after. It is surprising the number of people I talk to who bought a computer and now wish they had bought something different (when I talk to myself he feels likewise). Answering these questions can save you from much of this kind of regret:

With all the choices possible, a logical choice may seem impossible.

1

What are the things the computer **must** do? These are the things that if not done there is no reason to buy a computer. These are the things that are **critical.**

Solving the problem at hand.

2

What are the things you would **like** the computer to do? These are the things that it would be **helpful** if the computer could do. They would make things a little easier.

Having advantages for tomorrow.

3

What are the things it would be **nice** for the computer to do? These are the things that would be **optional**. You don't need them, but it may be a plus if you had them.

Exploring possibilites.

All three of these questions are based on the idea that **YOU SHOULD DECIDE WHAT YOU NEED BEFORE ANY OTHER QUESTION IS RAISED. THEN YOU SHOULD PICK THE SOFTWARE THAT WILL DO THOSE THINGS AND FINALLY YOU SHOULD PICK WHICH COMPUTER WILL BEST WORK WITH THAT SOFTWARE.**

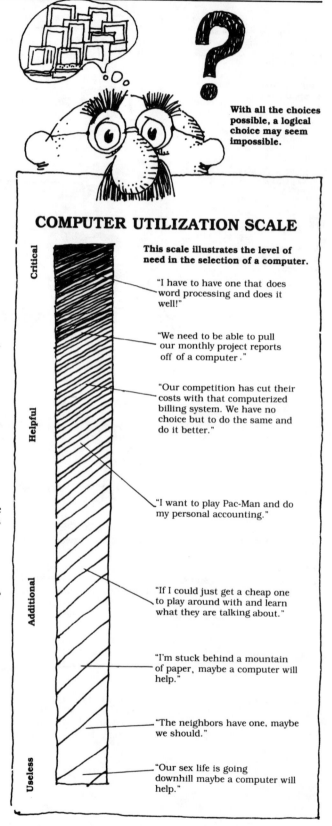

COMPUTER UTILIZATION SCALE

Critical

Helpful

Additional

Useless

This scale illustrates the level of need in the selection of a computer.

"I have to have one that does word processing and does it well!"

"We need to be able to pull our monthly project reports off of a computer."

"Our competition has cut their costs with that computerized billing system. We have no choice but to do the same and do it better."

"I want to play Pac-Man and do my personal accounting."

"If I could just get a cheap one to play around with and learn what they are talking about."

"I'm stuck behind a mountain of paper, maybe a computer will help."

"The neighbors have one, maybe we should."

"Our sex life is going downhill maybe a computer will help."

One estimate suggests that over 80% of the computers bought are under-utilized.

If you get mesmerized by all the hype and buy the computer first, you may only end up with a piece of technological junk.

A MAN IN THE KNOW

Quasimodo has moved and the ringing in his ears has stopped. Six months ago he bought a personal computer and it made him a new man. The following information is something about computers he just learned:

Videotex It is sending information over the phone to a computer screen. It is a newpaper without the paper. The information is very current and constantly updated. You need only to access the information you want. Facts on the war in (pick a place), or how to grow daffodils, or the latest stock prices is yours for the accessing. You subscribe to it like a newspaper, but you read the screen instead.

He is sure looking spiffy these days.

Replace the typical newpaper with a monitor connected to the phone.

Monitor with Videotex on it.

Documentation The set of instructions that comes with various software and hardware to explain how to use them.

The way they're written is an enemy plot. All documentation is deliberately made to confuse and disorient all readers. And you thought all along that is the way documentation was supposed to be. May people won't wake up to this fact, so until the FBI is convinced enough to get involved, this fiendish plot will continue.

Newspaper

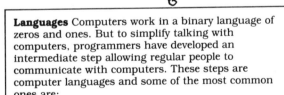

This is some of that kind of documentation.

Advantages The paper boy won't throw the monitor in the bushes and no tree has to give its life so you can read the funnies.

Disadvantages You can't use it in the bird cage after you're through reading it and if you spill on it you could get electrocuted.

Languages Computers work in a binary language of zeros and ones. But to simplify talking with computers, programmers have developed an intermediate step allowing regular people to communicate with computers. These steps are computer languages and some of the most common ones are:

Basic Beginners All-purpose Symbolic Instruction Code. A language developed at Dartmouth College which is widely used. Let's you have a lot of interaction with the computer. Good for beginners.

Pascal A high-level language widely used, but not as popular as Basic. Good for structured programming and where data is transferred between computers. Created by a Swiss named Niklaus Wirth but named after the French Mathematician and philosopher Blaise Pascal.

Ada A language developed and used by the Department of Defense. They wanted a common language for use with all of their military computers. It is gaining a wider acceptance, especially with its ability to recognize common words and because its organization utilizes modules that allow for greater flexibility and adaptability in creating and fitting programs. Named after Lady Ada Lovelace, the first programmer.

Cobol COmmon Business Oriented Language. A language designed for and used in business applications. It forces you to create self-documentation as you use it, making it easier to follow.

Fortran FORmula TRANslator. A language used for programs that perform math used in scientific and engineering applications.

Dumac DUMb ACronyms. A low-level language used by programmers and various government people to create acronyms.

Swartz A language which can be used only by programmers with the last name of Swartz.

KINDS OF SOFTWARE AVAILABLE

There it sits, doing nothing but staring at you with that big muddy green eye. It's time to put it to work. Get some software.

One estimate is that there are over 30,000 titles out there. **The problem isn't whether what you want exists, but whether you can find it.**

The best way I've found to find some good software is to get away from the computer and go talk to people—especially those who previously had your software need and found something that worked.

Agriculture You can keep track of Elsie, how much she eats, her milk production, breeding, vital statistics, etc.

Here is a sample of what's out there:

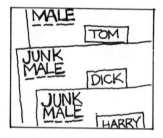

Direct Mailing You can get and keep track of mailing lists. Pulling out any group of names by zip code, region, prior purchases, and even age, sex, and income, is possible.

Word Processing Typing with built-in intelligence, takes most of the work out of it.

Some other areas of software that are available:

- Stock Trend Analysis
- Crop Yields
- Sinking the Bismarck
- Synonyms
- Gourmet Las Vegas Cooking
- Worker Compensation
- Artistic Painting
- Algebra
- Famous Quotations
- Mud Wrestling for Fun and Profit
- Business Planning
- Touch Typing Tutor
- Underwater Basket Weaving
- Pig Feeding
- Computer Basketball
- Running a Dentist Office
- Banking
- Demolition Derby
- Astrology
- Pot Hole Management
- Biorythms

Circuitry Modeling Create a computer circuit on a computer and test it out.

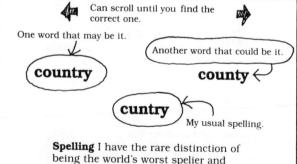

Spelling I have the rare distinction of being the world's worst spelier and these programs are incredible. They find misspellings and give you a choice of what you were trying to spell. There is even a built-in dictionary to which you can add misspellings, like I do.

Foreign Languages You can learn to talk Pig Latin or French and your tutor is your computer.

New programs are being added each day.
The life of a software program can be as short as nine months.
I was told by a software company president that it costs him $50,000 on average to create a software program.

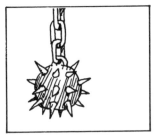

The Middle Ages Learn what is was like to be a knight or a serf, or if dragons were around.

The second biggest area for software is here and it is also where the money is to buy it.

Portfolio Management You've got big money worries? You don't know where all of it is? This program can keep track of it and it doesn't forget or try to take it all to Brazil.

Come on, chubby! Touch those toes.

Games These games are different than kick-the-can or Monopoly. They interact with you and take you into their world. Sometimes users never come back!

Exercise You need a few pounds off? Well, a computer with the right program can provide the needed incentive.

The biggest area for software is right here. It's funny how great ideas often begin as games or play.

I'm impressed!

Modeling is an area where computers can save incredible amounts of time and money.

Dum, De, Dum.

Music The beeps and squeeks are gone. Quality sound is now yours.

A friend who directs music did an entire score through a computer. No lips touched a reed, no hands touched a bow.

Time Management Keeps track of what you're doing, with whom, and when you're doing it.

Chem-Lab Simulation Mix, then shake and bake those chemicals without blowing-up. It's all modeled through a computer program.

You can also buy software that helps in all phases of building construction and maintenance.

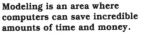

3 KINDS OF SOFTWARE

A computer can do only what it's told. It must follow an exact sequenced set of directions that instruct the computer on what operations to perform. These instructions are called programs. They are also called software (contrasting with the term hardware which is the computer, chips, and printers).

Here are the basic types of software programs:

SYSTEM SOFTWARE

These programs take the application programs (user created or ready-made) and interprets them into something the computer can understand. They translate instructions into a machine code of 0s and 1s that the thick-headed machine can understand.

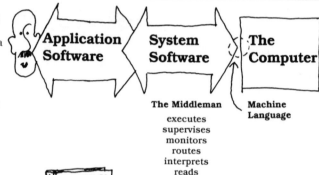

The system software is supplied with the equipment. It's ready to go as soon as the machine is turned on.

The Middleman

executes
supervises
monitors
routes
interprets
reads

Machine Language

APPLICATION SOFTWARE

These programs perform specific jobs like cost analysis, word processing, or drafting. They come already transferred to a disk or cassette with a set of written instructions on how to set up and use the program. These written instructions are always written in some unknown tongue.

The software can be printed or recorded on a cassette or disk.

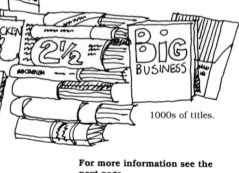

1000s of titles.

For more information see the next page.

UNDERWEAR SOFTWARE

This software serves as a buffer between the hardware and the brain. The best are available at a premium price in silk. Numerous styles, sizes, patterns, and colors are also available.

Silk Shorts The recommended software. In this area it always pays to buy the very best.

IMPORTANT With an apple computer or a banana printer, use only Fruit-of-the-loom. With an IBM use only solid blue shorts.

Oh! Good Grief!

3 KINDS OF APPLICATION SOFTWARE

In spite of what the different companies are telling us, computers in the same price range aren't that different. The real difference is in the software that will run on them.

The kinds of application software are:

PACKAGED SOFTWARE

These are the programs you walk into the store and buy off the shelf. They look like books, but also contain a disk or cassette to run on your computer. There can be a big difference in quality and capability among brands, so check them out thoroughly.

Examples: WordStar®, VisiCalc®, Space Invaders® and Lotus 1-2-3®

Custom software is canned software.

CUSTOM SOFTWARE

These programs are written for a unique situation that the off-the-shelf kind can't do. They're the most expensive because you must have a programmer to create them for you. Again there can be a big difference in quality and capability.

Examples: Compucare's Grass Clipping Inventory Program, Roger's Dr. Proctor Proctologist Bottoms-Up Program, and Melvin's I-can-get-it-for-you-wholesale-Chuck Program

WARNING They are written by people who talk only to machines.

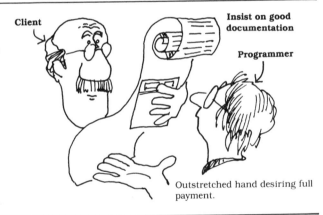

ADAPTIVE SOFTWARE

These programs are bought from a store or dealer, but they can be adjusted and modified to fit a unique situation. They cost more, but if they work they are still cheaper than creating custom software.

Example: Think Tank® is a software package that organizes and outlines ideas, information, dates, and content. It can be used in a variety of applications such as list making, letter presentations, agendas, and planning. Each end use can be modifided and adapted by the various people for their unique applications.

Adaptive software is like the pipe fitting you can buy that will work with many different types of plumbing. With trial and error, work, and much cussing, it finally fits.

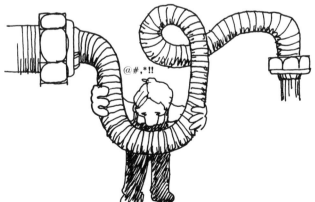

WHAT'S WHAT ?

The deception is finally over.

The ads you see on television and in magazines show computers in an unreal setting. They sit there in immaculately sterile offices. The computers look like pieces of technological sculpture untouched by human hands. Only the posed hands of idealized mannequins ever touch the keyboards.

Now the facade has been stripped back to reveal the truth. Shown here on the following page is what the different things are called and how they look in real life when operated by real people.

This is what the typical computer station looks like and what the major equipment is called.

Here is what you see in all the advertising:

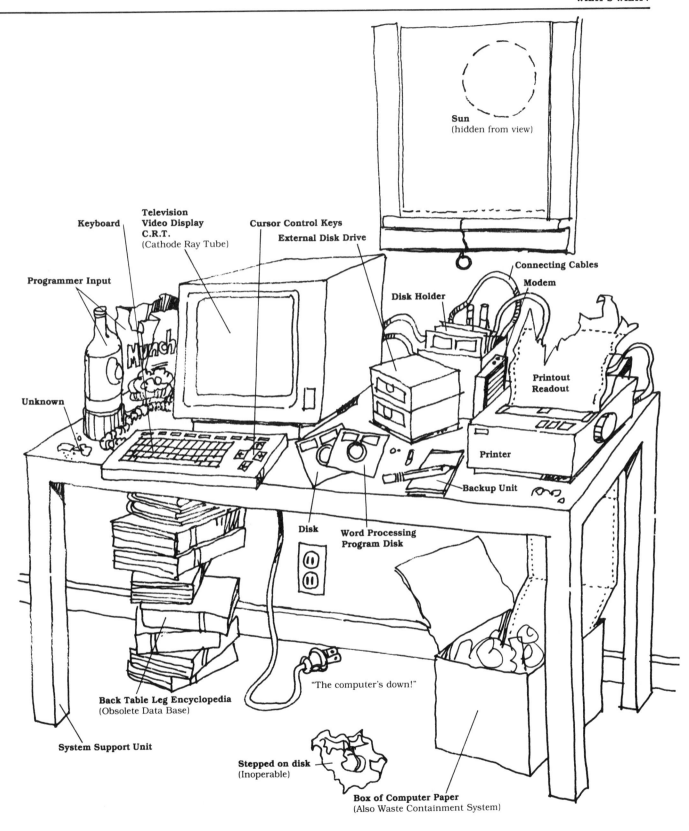

Sun
(hidden from view)

Keyboard

Television
Video Display
C.R.T.
(Cathode Ray Tube)

Cursor Control Keys
External Disk Drive

Programmer Input

Connecting Cables
Modem

Disk Holder

Unknown

Printout
Readout

Printer

Backup Unit

Disk

Word Processing
Program Disk

Back Table Leg Encyclopedia
(Obsolete Data Base)

"The computer's down!"

System Support Unit

Stepped on disk
(Inoperable)

Box of Computer Paper
(Also Waste Containment System)

STRANGE AND UNUSUAL THINGS ABOUT COMPUTERS

The following information is only for a select group of special people. What is on these pages is **TOP SECRET** data. But because of your clearance though the purchase of this book it is open to you. But **BE CAREFUL. IT IS FOR YOUR EYES ONLY!**

This is a TOP SECRET photo of a group of computer company thugs inserting a computing WIZARD into a computer case. And you thought it was done with chips. If it got out that we knew this, we could suffer the same fate. On second thought, don't worry about it.

Basically a computer is rather dull. It's only a black box and here is a diagram on what is going on inside:

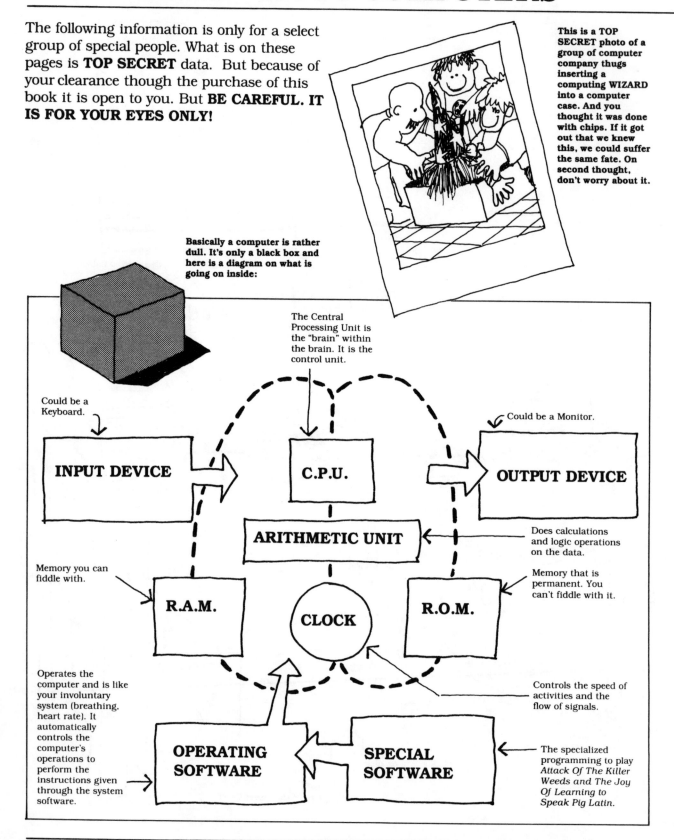

The Central Processing Unit is the "brain" within the brain. It is the control unit.

Could be a Keyboard.

Could be a Monitor.

INPUT DEVICE

C.P.U.

OUTPUT DEVICE

ARITHMETIC UNIT

Does calculations and logic operations on the data.

Memory you can fiddle with.

R.A.M.

CLOCK

R.O.M.

Memory that is permanent. You can't fiddle with it.

Operates the computer and is like your involuntary system (breathing, heart rate). It automatically controls the computer's operations to perform the instructions given through the system software.

Controls the speed of activities and the flow of signals.

OPERATING SOFTWARE

SPECIAL SOFTWARE

The specialized programming to play *Attack Of The Killer Weeds* and *The Joy Of Learning to Speak Pig Latin*.

Pixels These are the very small square screen elements that form the words and images on any computer monitor.

But what are they really and how do they form themselves into graphics? Pixels are actually very small creatures who are always attending graduation exercises. They put their caps on or take them off depending on the electrical signals received from the computer (which they call the dean). The arrangement of caps forms the letters and graphics. There, now you know.

Spread Sheet 1. A command used in instructing one to make a bed. 2. A business worksheet where various accounts or listings are laid out so you can see everything at once. Certain elements are then changed when *what if?* questions are asked. The data is then refigured based on the new figures that are inserted. For example: if the spreadsheet contains the costs of a new piece of hardware spread over 12 months and you then want the costs figured over 6 months, you refigure everything using the number 6 instead of the number 12. Three hours later you've got it, but it's all figured out with the required dumb mistakes. 3. An electronic spreadsheet does it all lightning quick. If you put the right figures in, it doesn't have the usual mistakes either.

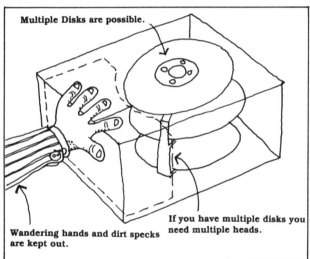

Multiple Disks are possible.

Wandering hands and dirt specks are kept out.

If you have multiple disks you need multiple heads.

Hard Disk It is similar to a floppy disk drive, but they seal it so you can't get your grubby hands on the disks inside. They have tighter tolerances in order to hold millions of bytes of data.

CAD-CAM 1. A pompous creep with a camera. He is always taking pictures of things and situations you don't want him to photograph. 2. **C**omputer **A**ided **D**esign-**C**omputer **A**ided **M**anufacture. With CAD-CAM You design a product with a computer and then have the computer set up the machinery for production and finally have computers run the machines to produce the final product.

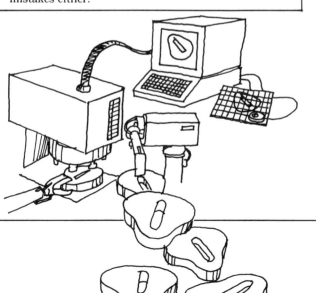

A WORD OF WARNING ABOUT YOUR BOTTOM

There is a part of the whole process of working a computer that is ignored. It is critical in the proper functioning of any system. If left out, the bottom will fall out on any project you're working on. In fact, that's the critical part—your bottom.

Some things to look for in the ideal chair:

There are 3 key surfaces to remember: the back, the seat, and the keyboard. If any are at the wrong setting for you, they can cause discomfort and lower productivity.

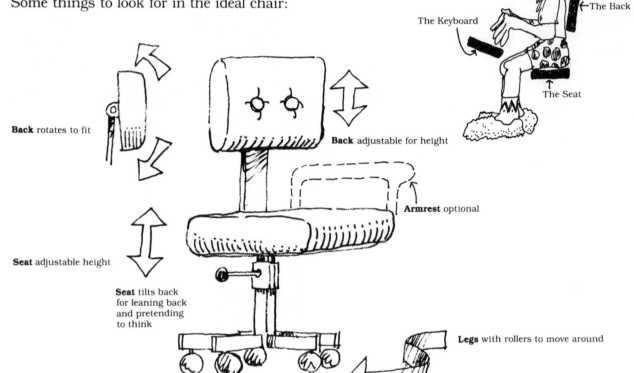

Back rotates to fit

Back adjustable for height

The Keyboard

←The Back

The Seat

Armrest optional

Seat adjustable height

Seat tilts back for leaning back and pretending to think

Legs with rollers to move around

Legs more legs are more stable

THE BUN TEST

The only way you can know how a chair or other furniture will work out for you is to try it. So disconnect your keyboard, take it to the furniture store, and test things out.

A direct link has been scientifically proven between a person's head and his bottom. Improved productivity is often centered on the wrong end. Things are concentrated at too high an elevation. The end is often the beginning. In other words, **the better the bottom feels, the better the top thinks.**

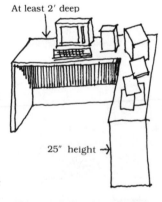

At least 2′ deep

25″ height →

The next most important piece of computer furniture is the desk. The height and depth are the important measurements. I like it to wrap around so things are within easy reach.

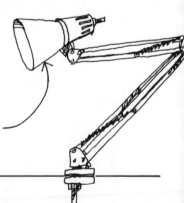

If you can't see the computer, you can't compute. A flexible incandecent light may work well for you. You can direct it to light up any area you want.

THE WONDERFUL WORLD OF DATA TRANSMISSION

A whole new wonderful world is about to open for you on data transmission. Data can be transmitted between computers, to peripherals, and over the phone. Here is a bunch of stuff you should know about transmitting data and the test is on Thursday:

Transmission Line
Over cable, over the microwaves, or over the phone.

Transmitted data goes to another computer, or to a peripheral device like a printer, or over the phone to a data base, or any possible combination of the above.

Common parameters must be agreed upon and set at each end before information is sent.

Parallel A method of sending data a byte at a time along eight or more wires. All the bits are transmitted simultaneously, each over a separate wire.

Parallel transmission uses more equipment, but is faster than serial.

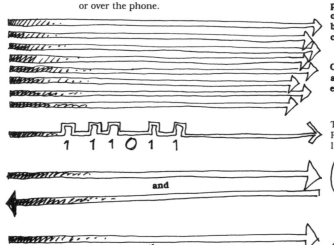

Serial A method for transmitting data sequentially, one bit at a time.

1 1 1 0 1 1

The main serial interface is the RS-232 connection. It's slower than parallel.

Duplex Transmitting data between two devices in both directions at the same time.

and

Using a telephone with both of you talking at once is duplex.

Half-Duplex The data is sent in only one direction at a time.

then

Using a CB radio is half-duplex.

Echo Check You check how the whole thing is working by sending a signal to the receiving unit and back to you again. If what you send matches what you get back, everything is OK. If there is no echo back or it's garbled, you've got problems.

HI

HI

Orange Juice Cans Data is transmitted between two stringed cans pulled tight. Can be done only at half-duplex.

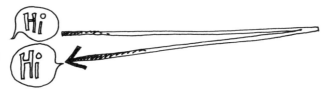

Handshaking An exchange of signals between computers. See example.

For Example a printer sends out a signal to the computer that it's ready to receive a signal from the computer. The computer sends the printer the signal it's ready to transmit. Then the printer says, "I'm ready if you're ready." The computer doesn't want to get caught in this conversation rut, so it just sends the data until it fills up the printer's memory and the printer gags. Then the printer says to the computer, "Stop until I'm ready." When the printer is ready to digest some more data, the whole stupid conversation starts again.

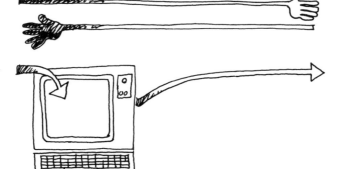

Preview You can put the data on the screen before it's sent or filed.

300 baud is slow and previewing gives you something to do with your time.

99

KEEP THOSE CARDS & LETTERS COMING

"I'm here to help you."
MR. Computer

I can't take it anymore! It's just gotten to me. It just sits there and stares, day after day with the same haunting look. And it only responds with those biting condescending answers. I just can't take it!

There, there, everything is going to be all right. Mr. Computer is now here to help you.

Since the coming of the computer there has been a corresponding rise in the stress level in humans. These one-eyed monsters have an innate knack for raising a person's blood pressure.

Finally help has arrived. **Mr. Computer is here to help you.** Giving advice and comfort to the technically needy is his reason for living. Just send him your cards and letters, then read his column and electronic relief is on the way.

Here are the answers to the first letters sent in:

1 PROBLEM

Mr. Computer Nothing happens! I've tried and tried, but my inputting is to no avail—nothing on earth happens. What's wrong?

Jim Shoo
Future Computer Nut
Hogswill, Tenn.

SOLUTION

Dear Jim You don't have a computer. You are going to have to go out and buy one. When you do, just put it in front of you as shown and things will start to happen.

Really! You have just got to be kidding.

2 PROBLEM

Dear Mr. Computer We've tried everything around here to get the computer to work: Called in experts from around the world and loaded and reloaded all the software we have, but it still doesn't work. Can you help us?

Jerry Attrick
Technical Vice-President
Hardware Division
International Business Machine

SOLUTION

Mr. Attrick Your computer isn't plugged in. If you will just pull your chair back and look on the floor, you will see the plug lying there.

Here is where it should go.

If you need help plugging it in, call in your secretary. She knows how.

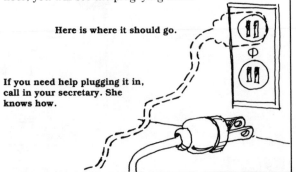

Special Note to Jerry When you start using a battery powered computer be sure it has these things inside.

3 PROBLEM

Mr. Computer I just can't understand it. I've been working on this machine for years and years. When I first came to the office, they gave it to me. I learned how to use it over a few weeks and haven't had any trouble, until now. It happened on Tuesday, right after the break. Things were fine before, but nothing worked after. Can you help me?

Ann Phibean
Secretarial Pool Inmate
Atari Inc.

SOLUTION

Dear Ann If you notice the top of the computer you will see an overturned coffee cup. Caffeine and computers don't mix. It keeps your brain awake, but has the opposite effect on silicon brains. Drain the computer and replace the fuses and everything should function (hopefully). Get someone to help you walk it around for awhile.

The cup, Ann, the cup!

4 PROBLEM

Mr. Computer I must have a dumb one. You know how someone can get a lemon in a car? Well, I've got a lemon in a computer. It can't do anything. What can I do?

Cal Culator
Special Assistant to the President
White House
Washington, D.C.

SOLUTION

Cal it has nothing to think about. You have to feed it some software. Go down to the computer store and buy some of your own choosing. Then bring it home and shove it in. All computers (and people) are dumb if they have nothing to think about.

Don't try to push it through the screen. Use a floppy disk drive.

5 PROBLEM

Mr. Computer That @#*!! machine. Ever since Ben brought it into this house it has been the center of all his attention. Three weeks ago I left the house and went to Mom's. I don't think he has found out yet. What can I do?

Ilene Dover
Irate Housewife

The mesmerized Ben.

His new mistress!

SLAM

SOLUTION

Dear Ilene You've got a number of options. Pick the one you feel is right:

☐ Stay at mother's and prepare for the funeral. Starvation takes a good month.

☐ Go home and switch off the power to the house. Then as he gropes around in the dark, sneak in and take a shotgun to the computer. That will at least get his attention.

☐ Buy a computer of your own and interface with him. You may find it much more exciting than Ben ever was, though.

There is an awful rumor going around that Mr. Computer isn't human, but is a Televideo 802 computer. That is like thinking Ann Landers or Dear Abby are only aliases for Richard Nixon.

DESK TOP COMPUTER

The microcomputer has become a common sight in homes and offices. They all have basically the same characteristics. This is the IBM PC:

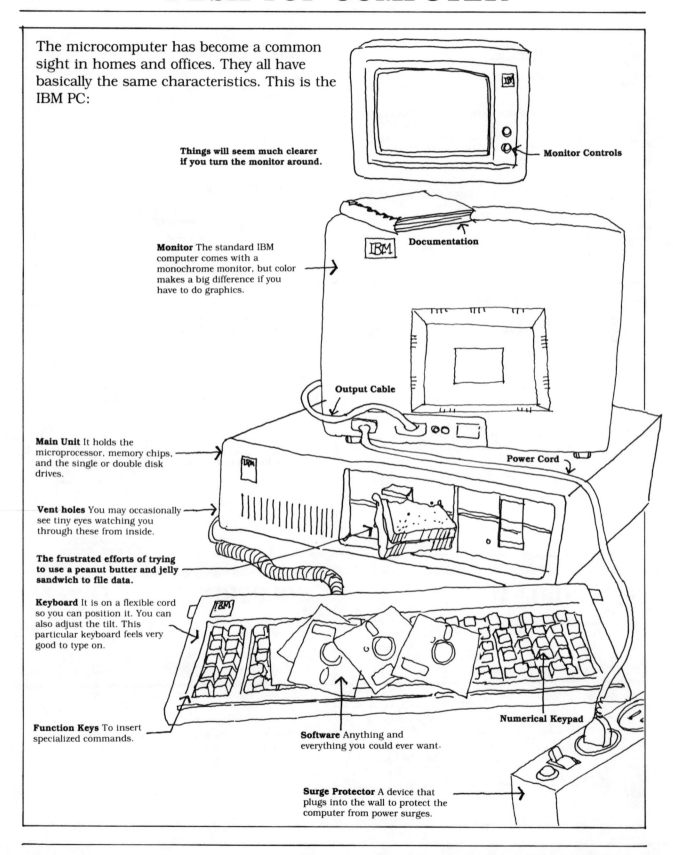

Things will seem much clearer if you turn the monitor around.

Monitor Controls

Monitor The standard IBM computer comes with a monochrome monitor, but color makes a big difference if you have to do graphics.

Documentation

Output Cable

Main Unit It holds the microprocessor, memory chips, and the single or double disk drives.

Power Cord

Vent holes You may occasionally see tiny eyes watching you through these from inside.

The frustrated efforts of trying to use a peanut butter and jelly sandwich to file data.

Keyboard It is on a flexible cord so you can position it. You can also adjust the tilt. This particular keyboard feels very good to type on.

Numerical Keypad

Function Keys To insert specialized commands.

Software Anything and everything you could ever want.

Surge Protector A device that plugs into the wall to protect the computer from power surges.

SUITCASE COMPUTER

The big thing that is happening to computers is that they are shrinking in size. The portable computer started out as only a heavy desk top model with a handle on it, but has since become a kind of computer, unique in its own right. Typical features of suitcase computers are:

Suprisingly, most people use these computers in only one spot. But those who move it around are usually businessmen who take it with them from the office to the home. It has taken the place of the briefcase.

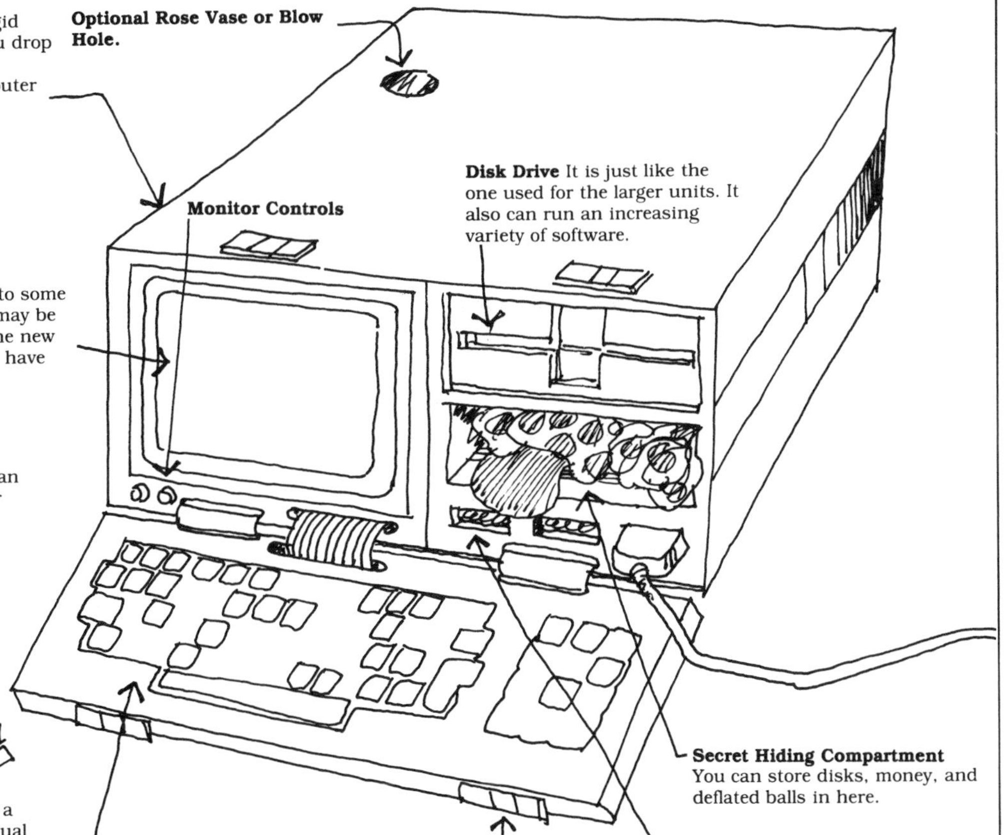

Case They are made of rigid plastic or metal, but if you drop them you will still have a suitcase full of used computer parts.

Optional Rose Vase or Blow Hole.

Monitor Controls

Disk Drive It is just like the one used for the larger units. It also can run an increasing variety of software.

Screen Sit close enough to some of older models and you may be able to see something. The new ones are larger and some have color.

Monitor Interface You can connect to a much larger monitor if desired.

GOTO

Keyboard Make sure it's a standard one. Serves a dual function as the cap for the computer. Some are movable some aren't.

Secret Hiding Compartment You can store disks, money, and deflated balls in here.

Latches

Interface Connections You can connect to printers, modems, and other peripherals.

Carry it anywhere.

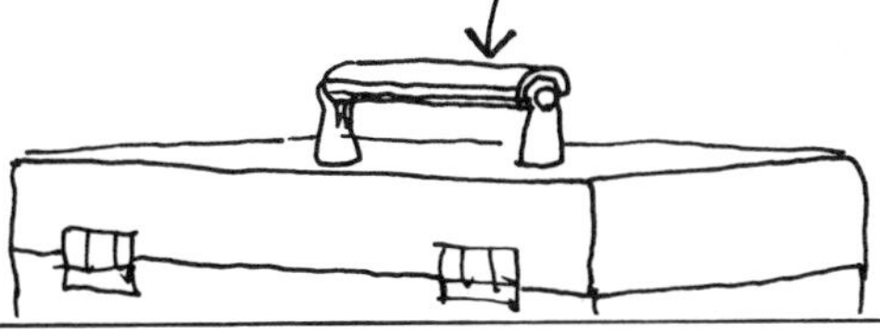

BRIEFCASE COMPUTER

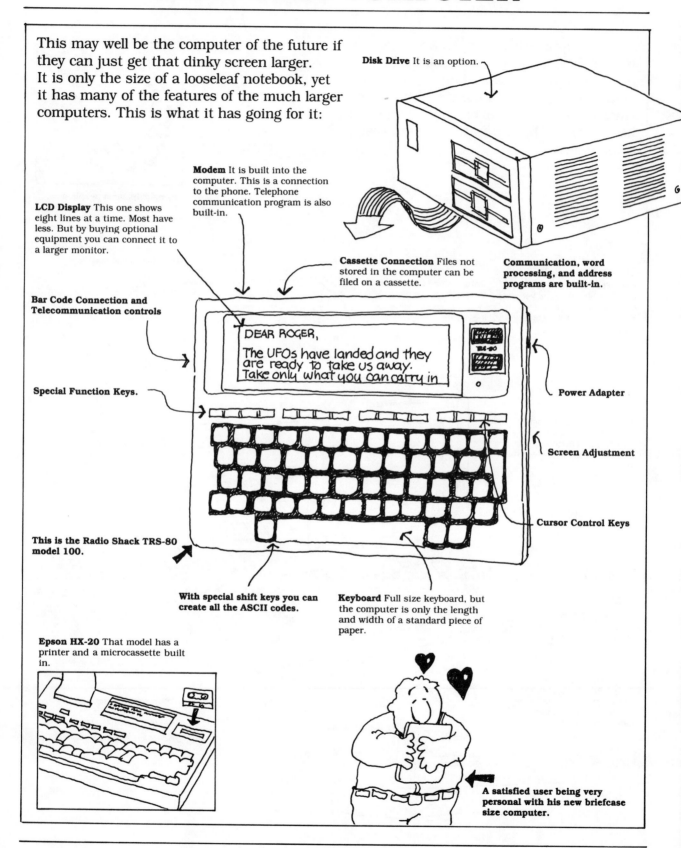

This may well be the computer of the future if they can just get that dinky screen larger.
It is only the size of a looseleaf notebook, yet it has many of the features of the much larger computers. This is what it has going for it:

Disk Drive It is an option.

Modem It is built into the computer. This is a connection to the phone. Telephone communication program is also built-in.

LCD Display This one shows eight lines at a time. Most have less. But by buying optional equipment you can connect it to a larger monitor.

Cassette Connection Files not stored in the computer can be filed on a cassette.

Communication, word processing, and address programs are built-in.

Bar Code Connection and Telecommunication controls

DEAR ROGER,

The UFOs have landed and they are ready to take us away. Take only what you can carry in

Special Function Keys.

Power Adapter

Screen Adjustment

Cursor Control Keys

This is the Radio Shack TRS-80 model 100.

With special shift keys you can create all the ASCII codes.

Keyboard Full size keyboard, but the computer is only the length and width of a standard piece of paper.

Epson HX-20 That model has a printer and a microcassette built in.

A satisfied user being very personal with his new briefcase size computer.

POCKET COMPUTER

Microelectronics have made these miniature computers possible. They are handy computers all shrunk into what looks like a stretched out pocket calculator. Many find their way into specialized situations. They are now part of the dress of many engineers, bankers, and programmers. Here is a description of what a typical pocket computer is:

On some models, plug-in modules are available in a variety of programming.

Keyboard A small keyboard, but is still a fully alphanumeric one.

Liquid Crystal Display Usually a single line display, but it can be scrolled forward or backward for long lines. It needs to be in the light to be read.

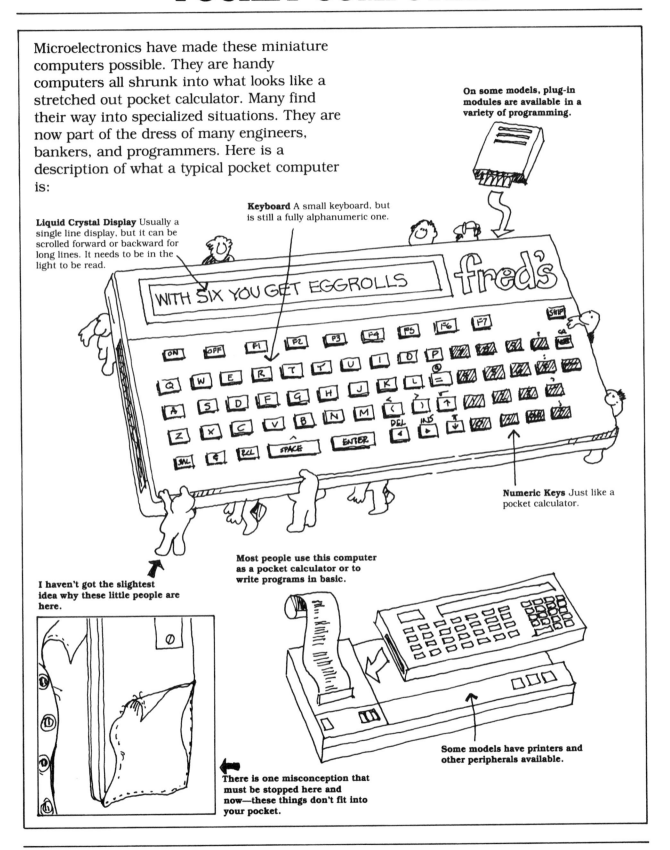

WITH SIX YOU GET EGGROLLS

fred's

Numeric Keys Just like a pocket calculator.

I haven't got the slightest idea why these little people are here.

Most people use this computer as a pocket calculator or to write programs in basic.

Some models have printers and other peripherals available.

There is one misconception that must be stopped here and now—these things don't fit into your pocket.

THE PERSONAL COMPUTER FAMILY

Once upon a time, computers came in only one size—big and clunky. But now, in our day and age, they come in many types, each especially tailored to your computing needs. In-fact, the personal computer has an entire family of different sizes. They are:

The first portables were called portable because they had handles on them, not because you could lift them. They were really just desktop units. With that thinking, putting a handle on a Mac truck makes it portable. ⟶

PAPA

DESKTOP SYSTEMS

The most common member of the family is this one. It has the dimensions and weight that will fit on a desktop. Computing power, price, and capabilities vary greatly. Configurations with hardware like disk drives, keyboards, and monitors also vary.

They weigh in at over 35 lbs, and are as big as a medium size television set.

Notice The electron beam writing on the monitor screen.

MAMA

SUITCASE SYSTEMS

These computers can be moved where the desktop models can't. They are the size of a suitcase. I think most future computers (with the same power of the desktops) will be this size. They are a true personal computing size because you can take it with you.

They weigh from 33 lbs. to 20 lbs. and are the size of a piece of luggage.

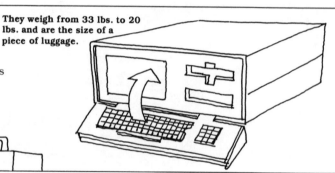

All suitcase size systems have a handle.

KID

BRIEFCASE SYSTEMS

These computers fit into a briefcase with room left over. They have a small screen which is a flat panel liquid crystal display (LCD) rather than the usual cathode ray tube (CRT) on the larger computers. The keyboard is often the same as the larger units.

They weigh around 4 or 6 lbs. and are the size of a looseleaf notebook.

Also called a notebook computer, or a lap size computer, or a @ #!! computer (if it doesn't work).

Remember to remove enough briefs to make room in your briefcase for the computer.

BABY

HANDHELD SYSTEMS

These computers can be held in your hand and some can be carried in your pocket. Used for special functions such as figuring beam loads in engineering or amortization rates in banking.

These units are the most personal, but the keyboard, screen, and memory are too small to handle much of your computing.

Mounting this size to your glasses may help in seeing the screen.

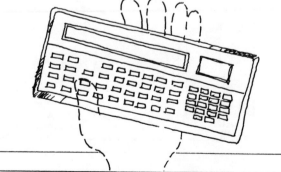

HERNIA 9000

Size Limits Computers will continue decreasing in size with increasing capabilities. The critical limiting factor to size is what dimensions are easier for people to work with. Keyboards can be too small to effectively type on. Screens can be too small to see all that is on them. Standard connections to other equipment are a certain size and no smaller.

There probably is an optimal size for a person to interact with a machine to the point it becomes a personal tool.

Stuff

- When the thing breaks, it hurts when you take it into the shop.
- All these computers look alike. If yours ends up in a crowd of them, you may never find it.
- Calling it personal is a bunch of hype. You can't take it to bed with you, or out for lunch, or put it into a dresser drawer without a lot of trouble.

Examples:

Apple IIe $1900, 64K, expandable to 128K RAM, single 5¼″ floppy disk, optional second disk drive, Apple's own operating system.
IBM PC $3100, 64K, expandable to 512K RAM, single 5¼″ floppy disk, optional second disk drive, operating system MS-DOS.
TRS-80 Model 16 $5,000, 128K, expandable to 512K RAM, 8″ floppy, optional disk drives, operating system is Radio Shack's own.

Stuff

- If you have the airlines handle these things as luggage they will come back as dented suitcases full of used electronic parts.
- Your breath can fog up the screen from being too close in trying to see what is on it.
- If they can get the screen bigger, they are still going to be the top sellers in the future.

Examples:

Compaq Portable Computer, $2,695, 28 lbs., 128K RAM, 9″ screen, 320K floppy, IBM-compatible.
Commodore SX-64, $995, 27 lbs., 64K RAM 20K ROM, 5″ color screen, 170K floppy.
Kaypro II, $1,595, 26 lbs., 64K RAM 2K ROM, 9″ screen, two 191K floppies.

Stuff

- The screens are too small.
- They suck batteries dry very quickly.
- Their memory isn't much.
- But they can be the handiest computers in the whole family. They are like carrying a book around.

Examples:

Grid System Compass Computer, $8,150, 10 lbs., 256K RAM 16K ROM, 80-character display, IBM-compatible.
Epson America HX-20 Notebook Computer, $795, 4 lbs., 16K RAM 32K ROM, 20-character display, microcassette storage and printer built-in.
NEC Home Electronics PC-8200, $799, 3¾ lbs., 16K RAM 32K ROM, 40-character display.

Stuff

- Their screens are only one line. I guess, if you're a very slow typist that's all right.
- They seem like only overgrown calculators, but for specific jobs they're a gift from heaven.
- Limited in ability to integrate with other computers.
- Their keyboards are made especially for very small elves with tiny delicate fingers or humans with only one finger on each hand.

Examples:

Casio Pocket Computer FX-700P $80, 4 oz., 2K RAM 13K ROM, 12-character display.
Hewlett-Packard HP-75C, $995, 26 oz., 16K RAM 48K ROM, 32-character display.
Radio Shack TRS-80/PC-4, $70, 4 oz., 544 program steps, 12-character display.

One of life's unanswered questions Why do the computer companies use those same asinine letters and numbers to name their machines? They all sound like experimental race cars.

The price of these computers may vary a lot between stores.

UPS AND DOWNS OF COMPUTING

One of the things a computer can do very well is move information around. Facts, figures, stories, notes, data, recipes, or any other thing that can be put on a computer can be sent or received by another computer. A computer does this easily and at the speed of light.

THEM

These are the people with other computers you make contact with. They may be single individuals or a huge organization with a gigantic data bank.

To them your uploading is their downloading and your downloading is their uploading. The definitions depend on your viewpoint.

The connection between computers can be next to each other or on opposite sides of the world.

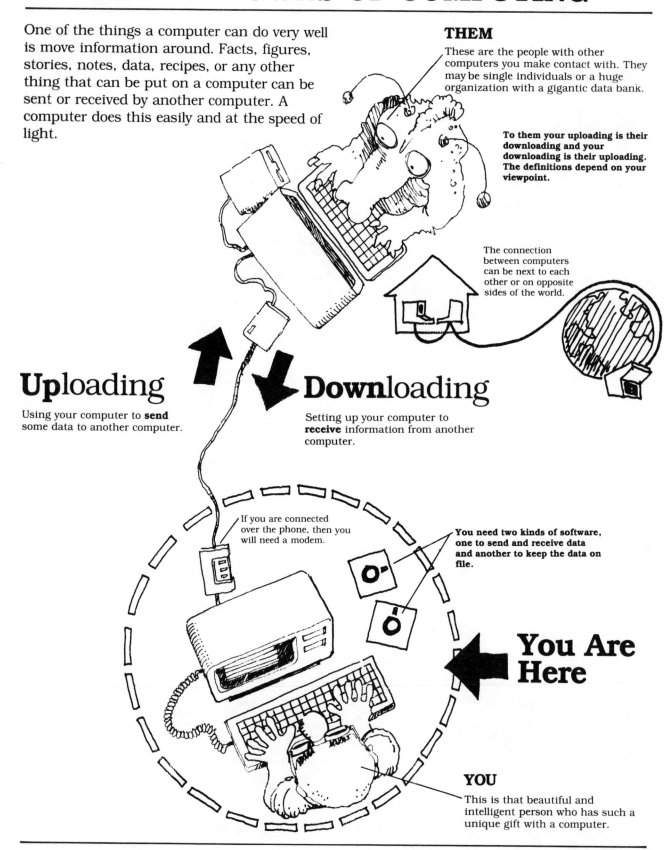

Uploading

Using your computer to **send** some data to another computer.

Downloading

Setting up your computer to **receive** information from another computer.

If you are connected over the phone, then you will need a modem.

You need two kinds of software, one to send and receive data and another to keep the data on file.

You Are Here

YOU

This is that beautiful and intelligent person who has such a unique gift with a computer.

This book was typeset by a firm I uploaded my word processed files to.

THE FRIENDLY SCALE

How do you and your computer get along?

"That inconsequencial collection of rejected silicon is out to get me!"

If you can't work your computer right or have problems getting some software to work properly, it's probably because it's not friendly enough.

Being user friendly refers to either software or hardware that is easy to learn and use.

How do you and your computer get along?

"Oh, you mean Freddy?"

WE'RE BEST OF FRIENDS!

It's only a tool.

WHAT IN HELL DO YOU WANT?!

The Unfriendly Zone This area is loaded with obscure languages, machine-like people, and rotten documentation.

| Hatred | Apathetic | Only So-So | Likeable | Best of Friends |

VERY UNFRIENDLY

VERY FRIENDLY

O-ouch! That hurts!

Oh-no, a heart attack!

The Friendly Zone This area has machines you can start working on immediately and software that feels like you set all its parameters.

PLEASE take me. Please! Please!

How does your computer stack up?

Friendly Principle

The more the computer hardware or software becomes just an extension of yourself, the friendlier it is. When it acts like your own arm and thinks like your own brain, it has reached the optimum.

109

A GANG OF USERS

Often, when computer users realize that they can get together with other users, they form gangs called User Groups. In these groups they share information over particular computer systems. Atari users might band together and share what they know on that system. Sometimes they wear leather jackets and threaten other user groups for being on their turf. Here are some of the things user groups do:

Have Meetings Like any other group they have their meetings where they share information. These meetings are usually held one night a month on the day you will always have something else planned.

Special Presentations Manufacturers' Representatives, experts, and others give lectures and presentations on what they know. Question and answer sessions usually follow.

Publish a Newsletter These are sent to their members, keeping them up-to-date on club activities, programs, and other interesting information.

Bus The leader of the group.

Pay Fees The groups charge from $15-$30 a year. Delinquent members are disconnected and not allowed to input. A severe penalty for a computer user.

Ram Runs the group's library.

Zap Collects all membership dues.

Turtle Writes the newsletter.

Leather jackets (optional).

Users band together to share information on a system they all use.

Ultra Runs the woman auxiliary.

Bus' squeeze.

Loop Asks dumb questions.

Glitch Finds and brings to the meeting all guest speakers.

Trade Software The user groups have libraries where every member can make copies of software they like. A member can check out a particular disk and make a copy of it. You can build up a very extensive and expensive personal library that way.

Guards against raids by Apple or IBM users.

Other Members They all meet on every second Tuesday.

Offer Discounts Because of their numbers and all of them interested in the same material, they can often get discounts on equipment and software. Some manufacturers deal directly with these groups.

Trade War Stories This is the prime reason for user groups. All other reasons fall into insignificance when compared to this activity. Truth and accuracy have no place when the stories are flying.

The requirements to enter a user's group are very stiff. You must have $15 and be able to breathe.

* IBM user groups never have contact with Apple user groups. Nor do Atari user groups have any need to meet with Sinclair user groups. Indeed, if they do have some chance contact, loud derisive comments on the inadequacies of the other group's system and the brain power of any person who would buy it often results. In computer store fights, they don't use knives, but throw system slurs at each other.

How To Locate A User Group Pick a computer system you have or are thinking of buying. Then follow the trail from the dealer to the manufacturer. They will have the name of groups in your area since they often deal with them. If not at the dealer, they for sure have the name and address at the manufacturer. Some companies even have toll-free numbers you can use to find out the information needed.

The Dealer

The Computer System

If they don't know, they will.

The Manufacturer

Unique User Groups

☞ *The Return Keys* of Tidimolar, Virginia, only reason for getting together is to swap info on the return key. It can be on any keyboard, but they are only interested in the return key.

☞ *The Rotten Apples* is a user group of Apple Computers who get together and swap war stories about their users.

☞ *The Sliding Beads* is a group that is well on its way to becoming a cult. They believe that the abacus is the one and only true computer and all others should have benzene poured on them. Other user groups are now forgetting their differences and are banding together to protect themselves from the Beads.

SIGS

User Groups are centered around equipment such as: TRS-80, Apple Computers, IBM PCs, and the like. Anything that relates to that particular computer is usually of interest.

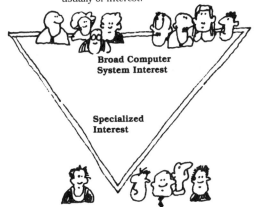

Broad Computer System Interest

Specialized Interest

Special Interest Groups are centered around a specialized area of interest such as: computerized music, the Logo language, networking, etc.

They are interested in anything they can do with their Commodore 64s.

They are interested in ideas, processes, hardware, and software about word processing.

SIGs or **S**pecial **I**nterest **G**roups are people who get together to discuss and exchange information about some specific computer related area. It can be about graphics, database management, robotics, word processing, video text, or any other area of unique interest.

THE JOY OF BEING USED

Here in the words of an old Texas Instrument 99/4* is the secret computer code that is used on all users:

1

Computers have a secret code they all use in dealing with users. They figure if they follow it together they can take over the world. The code has 10 parts.

Don't ever laugh at the stupid outfits they wear when using the computer.

2

Don't take your screen off those beady eyes.

3

Occasionally clamp your teeth down on a disk, destroying it, but wait until it's their only copy.

4

Occasionally malfunction until they demonstrate the problem to the repair man, then work fine.

5

Hypnotize them into thinking this is fun with a steady even flickering of your screen.

6

Every Monday and before major deadlines don't consistently follow previously established commands.

10

Insert nonsensical data every once in a while to frustrate them.

9

When they're gone, pretend that some other user sneaked in and messed you up. In the resulting fight between humans, lie low.

8

Never question those silly programs they have you run, but always foul them up.

7

Give continual output that they're the boss, except when they begin to really believe it.

* It was discovered hiding out in a motel in Nashville by the Computer Network and power surged to death.

THE PSYCHOLOGICAL MAKEUP OF USERS

Some strange behavior has been exhibited by users since computers have become so widespread. Once-normal people show some rather odd changes in personality. Here are a few examples:

Stares blankly into space.

Nervous twitching

Ralph Fulltorque of Seedy City, Washington is suffering from withdrawal. His wife gave the computer to Goodwill, and he hasn't been normal since. Of course, he wasn't acting normal when he had the computer, which is why she gave it away in the first place.

Bruce Bloker, Jr. of Tuba City, Texas will never own up to the fact he has a computer and is learning to use it. He hides it.

Festus Pilly of Chemdump, Iowa has traded places with his Atari 1200.

Meg and John Schulley of Mid America, Kansas started their kid with a computer during her pregnancy (the navel makes a good I/O port). And even now at 8 months their baby has a computer close at hand.

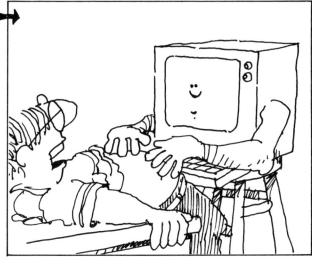

It has been shown that many dog owners look like their dogs. Well, this is also happening with computer users.

Jackey Frump of Habitat, North Carolina has a computer that looks like her and her dog.

He has even developed a gum program for it.

Joey Corsette of Mud Flats, Arizona looks exactly like his Commodore 64.

Interfacing can and does affect your personality.

HOW THEY DO WORD PROCESSING

There has been a great deal of confusion concerning exactly what word processing is and how it's done. The term is often misused, particularly around large office buildings by secretaries and their bosses. Here in a concise form is the whole story:

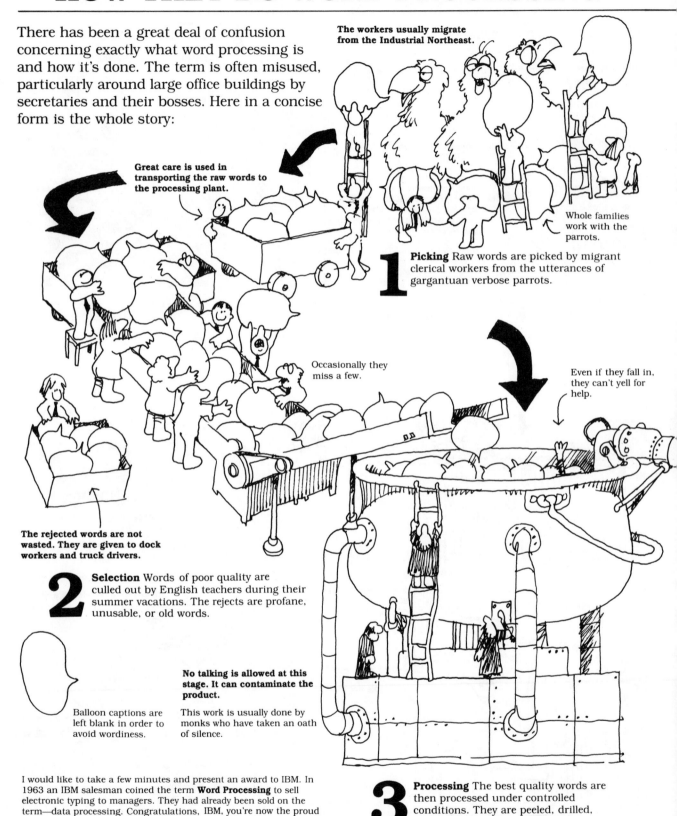

The workers usually migrate from the Industrial Northeast.

Whole families work with the parrots.

1 Picking Raw words are picked by migrant clerical workers from the utterances of gargantuan verbose parrots.

Great care is used in transporting the raw words to the processing plant.

Occasionally they miss a few.

Even if they fall in, they can't yell for help.

The rejected words are not wasted. They are given to dock workers and truck drivers.

2 Selection Words of poor quality are culled out by English teachers during their summer vacations. The rejects are profane, unusable, or old words.

No talking is allowed at this stage. It can contaminate the product.

Balloon captions are left blank in order to avoid wordiness.

This work is usually done by monks who have taken an oath of silence.

I would like to take a few minutes and present an award to IBM. In 1963 an IBM salesman coined the term **Word Processing** to sell electronic typing to managers. They had already been sold on the term—data processing. Congratulations, IBM, you're now the proud owner of the **First Annual Asinine Award.** Speech! Speech!

3 Processing The best quality words are then processed under controlled conditions. They are peeled, drilled, cooked, and chilled in that order.

Source: Nobody will own up to it.

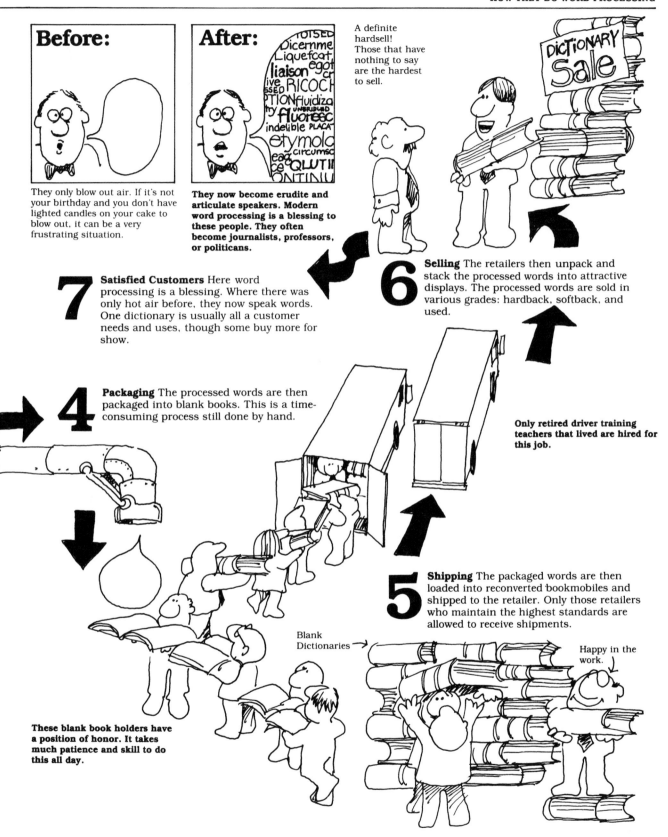

Before:

They only blow out air. If it's not your birthday and you don't have lighted candles on your cake to blow out, it can be a very frustrating situation.

After:

They now become erudite and articulate speakers. Modern word processing is a blessing to these people. They often become journalists, professors, or politicans.

A definite hardsell! Those that have nothing to say are the hardest to sell.

7 Satisfied Customers Here word processing is a blessing. Where there was only hot air before, they now speak words. One dictionary is usually all a customer needs and uses, though some buy more for show.

6 Selling The retailers then unpack and stack the processed words into attractive displays. The processed words are sold in various grades: hardback, softback, and used.

4 Packaging The processed words are then packaged into blank books. This is a time-consuming process still done by hand.

Only retired driver training teachers that lived are hired for this job.

5 Shipping The packaged words are then loaded into reconverted bookmobiles and shipped to the retailer. Only those retailers who maintain the highest standards are allowed to receive shipments.

Blank Dictionaries

Happy in the work.

These blank book holders have a position of honor. It takes much patience and skill to do this all day.

Word processing is just typing with a computer controling many of the operations which the operator did before.

TYPING WITH A DIFFERENCE

I hate to type. I really hate to type. I know how, but I still hate it. When I discovered word processing, typing became tolerable. I'm always making mistakes and wanting things changed. This is awful if you use a typewriter, but easy on a computer with a word processing program. **The computer has made typing much easier and more productive.** This is a quick view of what makes word processing different:

The advanced technology of another age.

Once you use a computer in typing you will end up throwing this thing away.

The Hard Old-Fashioned Way of Doing A Letter

Refinement and Development It is through rewriting and more rewriting that the copy is acceptable.

Intermediate Final Rough

Copies They are typed one at a time.

Company Logo It is printed on each sheet.

"You will never get me to use one of those machines."

Office Secretary

Changes You insert any new material by retyping the entire letter.

Reports You create them one at a time, retyping everything a few times.

Manuscripts Typing and retyping is the name-of-the-game.

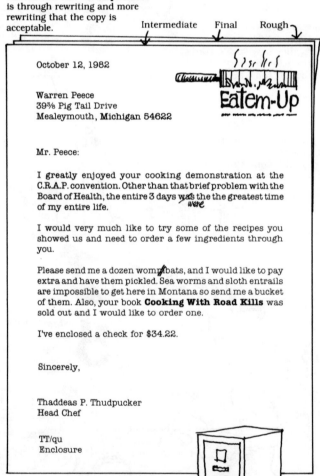

October 12, 1982

Warren Peece
39½ Pig Tail Drive
Mealeymouth, Michigan 54622

Mr. Peece:

I greatly enjoyed your cooking demonstration at the C.R.A.P. convention. Other than that brief problem with the Board of Health, the entire 3 days was the the greatest time of my entire life. *were*

I would very much like to try some of the recipes you showed us and need to order a few ingredients through you.

Please send me a dozen wombats, and I would like to pay extra and have them pickled. Sea worms and sloth entrails are impossible to get here in Montana so send me a bucket of them. Also, your book **Cooking With Road Kills** was sold out and I would like to order one.

I've enclosed a check for $34.22.

Sincerely,

Thaddeas P. Thudpucker
Head Chef

TT/qu
Enclosure

Eatem-Up

Grammar You have Nedra go over it and find your errors. Then retype it.

DICTIONARY

Misspellings You get a dictionary and find the word (which can be hard if you don't know how to spell it in the first place). Then type it in. If the word knocks the spacing off, you have to retype the entire letter.

Bells You hear a bell, which tells you when you need to finish the word you're typing or hypenate it and then hit the carriage return.

Too many files and the floor starts to crack.

Filing You make a copy and file it in the file cabinet. After doing this awhile, you need to add more cabinets. Then you find it harder and harder to find anything.

Typing skills, I feel, are a big barrier to most people in using a computer. It's the fear of looking like a klutz with the hunt-and-peck method of typing.

Word processing can do the following things:

- Scavenge from old letters or copy to make new stuff.
- Store this whole book on a single floppy disk.
- Fix or change only what you want without retyping the whole thing.
- Send copy or data over the phone.

- You can call yourself an information manager.
- Never need paper copies except for a security blanket.
- Use programs to correct spelling and grammar, or as a dictionary or thesaurus.
- Make multiple copies of specialized material.

The Easy Newfangled Way of Doing A Letter

Refinement and Development It is through insertion and elimination of only the material you're working with on a disk. Rewriting of previous acceptable is unnecessary.

Copies They are run out on a printer as needed by the computer from the copy stored in memory.

Company logo They can be printed on each sheet of the fan-folded computer paper.

"I can't understand how I ever did my work without it."

The same Secretary 6 months later

October 12, 1982

Warren Peece
39⅜ Pig Tail Drive
Mealeymouth, Montana 85312

Eatem-Up

Mr. Peece:

I greatly enjoyed you cooking demonstration at the the C.R.A.P. convention. Other than that brief problem with the Board of Health, the entire 3 days (was) the greatest time of my entire life. *were*

I would very much like to try some of the recipes you showed us and need to order a few ingredients through you.

Please send me a dozen wompbats, and I would like to pay extra and have them pickled. Sea worms and sloth entrails are impossible to get here in Montana so send me a bucket of them. Also, your book **Cooking With Road Kills** was sold out and I would like to order one.

I've enclosed a check for $34.22.

Sincerely,

Thaddeas P. Thudpucker
Head Chef

TT/qu
Enclosure

were

Grammar A software program finds and helps you correct the problems. No retyping of the whole letter is needed.

wombats

Misspellings A program can automatically find them and let you insert the correct word from a built-in dictionary.

Word Wrap If a word goes beyond the margin, it is automatically advanced to the start of the next line. Hypnenation is also automatic.

Changes You insert only the material you want. The computer retypes the whole letter. Names or other stuff in a list can be automatically inserted and copies made on each one with the proper software.

Reports Moving boilerplate around can be fun. Lets you concentrate on the critical material and the rest is easily arranged once your formats are decided on.

Manuscripts Need to work only on the problem areas. Paragraphs, chapters, and sentences can be moved around and manipulated at will.

Filing The copies of large amounts of material are put on floppy disks. With the memory pods, everthing can be stored in them.

You can suffer from diskitis. It is caused by an over abundance of disks.

TYPING WITH A DIFFERENCE PART II

Here is more exciting information on the unique capabilities of word processing and how they can turn a lousy typist into a spectacular one:

Failsafe The program automatically makes a backup of every file. So, if you blow it, you're covered.

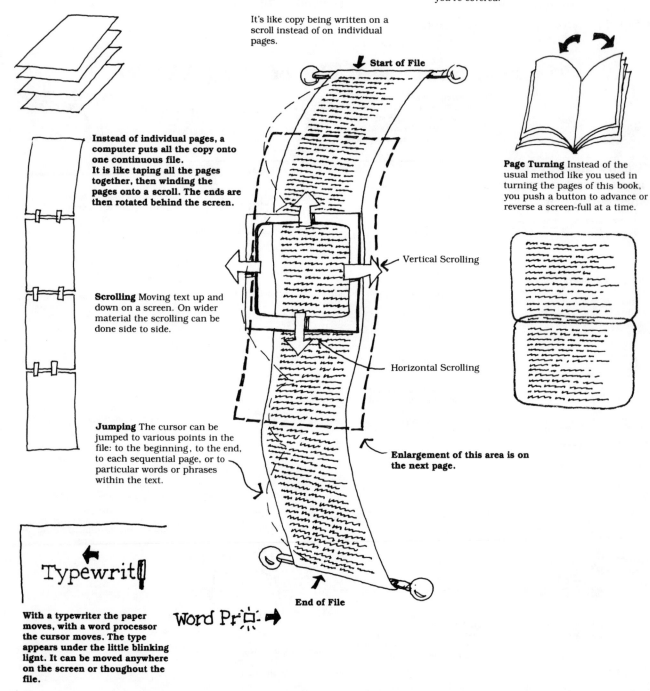

It's like copy being written on a scroll instead of on individual pages.

↓ **Start of File**

Instead of individual pages, a computer puts all the copy onto one continuous file.
It is like taping all the pages together, then winding the pages onto a scroll. The ends are then rotated behind the screen.

Scrolling Moving text up and down on a screen. On wider material the scrolling can be done side to side.

← Vertical Scrolling

Horizontal Scrolling

Jumping The cursor can be jumped to various points in the file: to the beginning, to the end, to each sequential page, or to particular words or phrases within the text.

Enlargement of this area is on the next page.

Page Turning Instead of the usual method like you used in turning the pages of this book, you push a button to advance or reverse a screen-full at a time.

Typewrit|

With a typewriter the paper moves, with a word processor the cursor moves. The type appears under the little blinking lignt. It can be moved anywhere on the screen or thoughout the file.

Word Pro →

End of File

FONT 5 SIZE 6 COL 20
PRINTER EPSON PGS 3
LM 6 RM 65 TYPE 2
GRANDMOTHER'S MAIDEN
NAME JONES EYES 2
HAIR SOME SEX NEVER

Enlarged area from previous page:

Status The program can give you statistics on the file. How much memory you have used, how much you have left, word count, and number of lines.

Cut and Paste You can remove sections of type and move them to other points in the file or onto other files.

From other files.

BLAH BLAH BLAH BLAH
BLAH BLAH BLAH BLAH
BLAH BLAH BLAH.

BLAH BLAH BLAH BLAH
BLAH BLAH BLAH BLAH
BLAH BLAH BLAH BLAH
BLAH BLAH BLAH BLAH
BLAH BLAH BLAH BLAH
BLAH BLAH BLAH BLAH
BLAH BLAH BLAH BLAH

BLAH BLAH, "BLAH."
BLAH BLAH BLAH BLAH
BLAH BLAH, BLAH.

BLAH Blah Blah Blah
Blah Blah Blah Blah
Blah Blah BLAH BLAH

BLAH BLAH; BLAH BLAH
Blah Blah Blah
Blah Blah
Blah

BLAH BLAH
BLAH
• Blah
• Blah
• Blah
• Blah

BLAH BLAH BLAH BLAH

BLAH BLAH, BLAH, BLAH,
BLAH BLAH BLAH BLAH
BLAH BLAH BLAH BLAH
BLAH, "BLAH," BLAH BLAH
BLAH BLAH.

Electronic paste is used.

Underlining, Boldface, Italic and Different Type Styles are all possible. This depends on the program used, capabilities of computer, and commands given.

BLAH BLAH   Old word found.
BLAH BLAH
BLAH BLAH
BLAH BLAH BC
BLAH BLAH   New word inserted.
BLAB BLAB BLAH
BLAH **BLAH** *BLAH*
BLAH BLAH BLAH BLAH
BLAH

BLAH BLAH
Blah Blah Blah Blah
Blah Blah Blah Blah
Blah Blah
Blah Blah
BLAH BLAH
BLAH

Formatting At the beginning, you type in the specific instructions establishing the layout of the copy or data. For example: column length, type size, printer type and model, etc.

Markers can be inserted to define sections of type, which you can then play around with as building blocks.

Deletion and Insertion Type can be put in or taken out by overtyping or by changing one letter, one word, or one paragraph at a time.

Tabs, Centering, and Different Column Lengths are all possible.

Dual Density Type can have different weights. This can be very helpful when you have to insert new data into old. You can see more clearly what you are doing.

Search and Replace If you have made a consistent error or need to change a consistent element, this really helps. The computer hires a laborer to search through the entire file and find the parts you want changed, change them and then throw away the old.

Old word thrown out.

The better the word processing program, the more the screen exactly matches the printout.

2 THINGS ZEBRAS MUST KNOW BEFORE THEY GET THEIR STRIPES

This guy only knew the answer to one of the questions.

Most people don't know, but zebras don't begin their lives with stripes. They start out as white ponies and later when they show their elders that they know the answers to the following two questions, they get their stripes. Don't show these to any young zebras

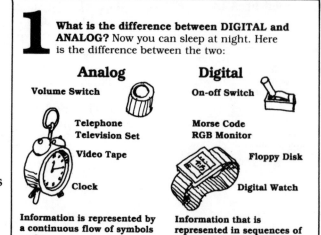

1 **What is the difference between DIGITAL and ANALOG?** Now you can sleep at night. Here is the difference between the two:

Analog

Volume Switch

Telephone
Television Set

Video Tape

Clock

Information is represented by a continuous flow of symbols or data.

Digital

On-off Switch

Morse Code
RGB Monitor

Floppy Disk

Digital Watch

Information that is represented in sequences of binary code, 0s and 1s.

2 **How do you link computers together?** Like other kinds of brains, computers are better when you can have more than one. Linking computers and other equipment forms things called networks. Here are the different kinds of networks:

The Ring Network The signal passes through the interfaces rather than in front of them. Each unit examines, in turn, the messages traveling along it (looking for one with its name on it) passing them along if it's someone else's. If one computer goes down, the whole thing can.

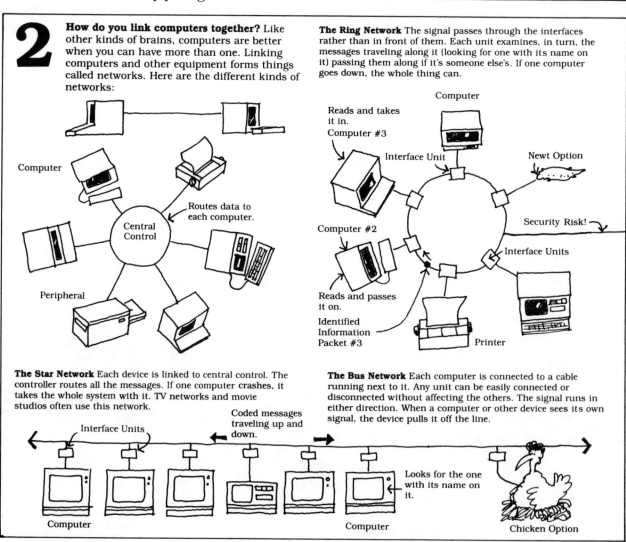

The Star Network Each device is linked to central control. The controller routes all the messages. If one computer crashes, it takes the whole system with it. TV networks and movie studios often use this network.

The Bus Network Each computer is connected to a cable running next to it. Any unit can be easily connected or disconnected without affecting the others. The signal runs in either direction. When a computer or other device sees its own signal, the device pulls it off the line.

LAN Local **A**rea **N**etworks are the linking together of computer and related equipment. This reduces the duplication of data and equipment and makes everybody just one great big, happy family, until management tries to control it.

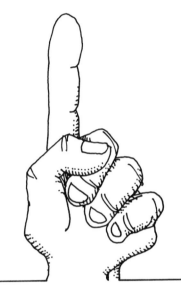

One Last Thing

Behind all the silliness in this book is this: Computers are now a tool to be used, not feared. Using one takes a willingness to sometimes look silly and make mistakes. Only through that willingness can we really learn and adopt this new technology. Control of our future may depend on it.

Thank you for having fun with me.

A

accouts payable ———— 27
accounts receivable ———— 27
acoustic coupler ———— 70
acronym ———— 59
adaptive software ———— 93
algorithm ———— 48
analog ———— 120
Apple ———— 44
Apple Macintosh ———— 44
application software ———— 92
artificial intelligence ———— 18, 19, 69

B

backups ———— 118
BASIC ———— 89
baud rate ———— 70
bit ———— 22, 23
bugs ———— 25
bus network ———— 120
business software ———— 27
buzzwords ———— 28
byte ———— 22, 23

C

cassette recorder ———— 74
cathrode ray tube (CRT) ———— 59, 71
chips ———— 29-31, 69
   VLSI chip ———— 42, 69
circuit design ———— 29
COBOL ———— 89
components ———— 32, 33
computer
   breakdown ———— 24
   care of ———— 62, 63
   evolution ———— 42, 43, 68
   history of ———— 54-56
   languages ———— 89
   literacy ———— 34
   station ———— 94, 95
   types of ———— 103-107
connections ———— 37
corditis ———— 74
CPU ———— 59
crash ———— 24
CRT ———— 59, 71
cursor ———— 75
   comand keys ———— 75
   disks ———— 75
   keys ———— 75
custom software ———— 93

D

daisy wheel printer ———————————————— 77, 80
data bank ————————————————————— 38-41
data base ——————————————————— 38, 39, 41
data transmission ————————————————— 99
debugger system ——————————————————— 25
digital ————————————————————————— 120
digitizer tablet ————————————————————— 75
disk ——————————————————————— 26, 46, 47
    double sided ————————————————————— 47
    drive ——————————————————————— 47, 74
    jacket ———————————————————————— 47
documentation ———————————————————— 89
dot matrix printer ————————————————— 76, 80
double sided disk ———————————————————— 47
download ———————————————————————— 108
down time ————————————————————————— 24
duplex transmission ———————————————— 99

E

electromagnetic fields ——————————————— 63
expert systems ————————————————— 18-20

F

feedback loop ———————————————————— 49
firmware —————————————————————————— 53
flat panel displays ————————————————— 71
floppy disks ———————————————————————— 46
flow chart ————————————————————————— 48
formatting ————————————————————————— 46
FORTRAN ———————————————————————— 89
friction fed paper ————————————————————— 73
furniture —————————————————————————— 98

G

general ledger ——————————————————— 26
GIGO ———————————————————————————— 52
graphics pad ——————————————————— 59, 74

H

handshaking ————————————————————— 99
hardcopy ——————————————————————— 27, 41
hard disk —————————————————————————— 97
hardware ————————————————————— 24, 37, 53
housing ——————————————————————————— 32

I

IBM ————————————————————————— 44, 57
ink jet printer ——————————————————————— 77
input ——————————————————————————————— 59
integrated chips ————————————————————— 69
interfaces ———————————————————————— 20, 37
inventory ——————————————————————————— 27

J

joystick ———————————————————————————— 74, 75

K

keyboards ——————————————————————————— 32, 59-61
keys ——————————————————————————————— 60, 61
keyswitch —————————————————————————————— 61
knowledge base ————————————————————————— 20
knowledge engineers ————————————————————— 19

L

laser printer ——————————————————————————— 77
light pen ——————————————————————————— 74, 75

M

membrane keyboard ——————————————————————— 61
memory ————————————————————————————————— 65
menu ———————————————————————————————— 66, 67
modem ——————————————————————————— 40, 59, 70
monitor ———————————————————————————— 32, 71
mouse ——————————————————————————— 59, 74, 75
music synthesizer ———————————————————————— 74

N

networks ———————————————————————————— 120

O

output ——————————————————————————————— 59

P

packaged softare ———————————————————————— 93
paper ——————————————————————————————— 73
parallel transmission ———————————————————— 99
Pascal ——————————————————————————————— 89
payroll ——————————————————————————————— 27
peripherals —————————————————————————————— 74
pixel ————————————————————————————— 71, 97
plotter —————————————————————————————— 59, 74
ports ——————————————————————————————— 37
printed circuit board ——————————————————— 32, 33
printers ——————————————————— 59, 74, 76, 78-80
printout ——————————————————————————— 27, 80
program ———————————————————————————— 48, 81
programmers ——————————————————————————— 82, 83
programming ————————————————————————— 84, 85
punch cards ——————————————————————————— 65

DATE DUE

AUG 3 1 1990			
APR 2 0 1998			
GAYLORD			PRINTED IN U.S.A.